EFFECTIVE
LEADERSHIP

EFFECTIVE LEADERSHIP

A Practical Guide to Leading Your Team to Success

Malcolm Bird

BBC BOOKS

Published by BBC Books,
a division of BBC Enterprises Limited,
Woodlands, 80 Wood Lane, London W12 0TT

First published 1992

ISBN 0 563 36416 5

Set in 10pt Times Roman by Ace Filmsetting Ltd, Frome, Somerset
Printed and bound in Great Britain by Clays Ltd, St Ives plc
Cover printed by Clays Ltd, St Ives plc

Contents

Introduction

This book is written for anyone who is responsible for the work of others.

Whether you supervise two clerks and the office boy or you are chief executive of a massive international organisation you need to be able to lead.

This means applying certain skills (which few, if any, people are born with) in order to motivate your people, get the best out of them and at the same time improve their working lives and improve the profit potential of your business. The skills required are the same whatever your role may be.

The book takes the findings of some of the management gurus of the past and translates them into practical, applicable and understandable actions. What, for example, did Abraham Maslow mean by 'fulfilment' as a motivating factor? Is it relevant to real-life managers?

Some tricky areas are also covered such as the extent to which money motivates. Will young Bloggs work more effectively if you give him a pay rise?

How to build a team, what 'communication' really means, how and why to delegate are other topics explained – all with real-life examples of successes and failures.

Getting these things right is the role of the manager as leader. Profit is the end-product and achieving it is entirely compatible with happy, motivated, properly led people.

The author makes no apology to the kick-'em-in-the-backside type of boss who will be horrified by the contents of this book.

In summary, the book is all about leading people instead of 'managing' them. It can be argued that leadership is one of the skills involved in managing but it seems that it is perhaps the most neglected skill. Much attention tends to be focused on products, customers, how to improve cash flow, or whatever. There is nothing wrong with doing so but without the backing of your staff, you will never achieve the best result. Paying more attention to leading pays off.

1 A Winning Smile is Not Enough

It is perhaps no accident that the *Concise Oxford Dictionary* makes no attempt to define 'leadership'. The dictionary does provide a definition of 'leader' but even this is restricted to functions such as leading an orchestra or membership of a government.

Leadership is difficult to define – at least in a few words. However, business people need to have a clear idea of what leadership is and, more especially, what constitutes *effective* leadership. In addition, business people need to know what they must do in order to be effective leaders.

Effective leadership can result in improved profits – or a profit rather than a loss.

Let us first dispose of two fundamental errors: the assertions that leaders are born and not made; and the opposing view that anyone can be trained to be an effective leader. The truth lies half-way between.

■ *The born leader*

There have been many effective leaders who have never had any formal training in leadership but this does not prove that leaders are born and not made. There are no little girls or boys who arrive in the world equipped with the ability to organise, plan, set objectives and satisfy the other requirements of the effective leader.

They may however be born with certain personality factors which are conducive to effective leadership once they have learned a great deal about people and the world about them.

One example is Nelson who was smart enough to realise that if, before a battle, he explained his plans to his captains he would have a better chance of success. He realised what should be obvious to any twentieth-century leader that if people understand the objectives and the plan then they will have at least an evens chance of achieving what the boss wants.

Nelson added this 'consultative' approach in the face of the contemporary belief that if a leader explained his ideas to his people he would diminish his authority.

Sadly, there are still so-called leaders (some of whom would claim to be born leaders) who, for one reason or another, fail to inform their people. They then blame the people when things go wrong.

The need to communicate (and how to do it) is one of the many skills which can be taught and which does not always come naturally to everyone who aspires to lead.

■ *It can all be taught*

If someone is born with the instincts of an angry Rottweiler and an I.Q. around 50 it is most unlikely that he or she can be trained to be an effective leader.

Such people can 'lead' by threats, bullying and brute force but the usual result is a disaster. Such people are often effective talkers and can be very persuasive.

Tom Lloyd, former editor of *Financial Weekly*, writing about Robert Maxwell in the *Daily Telegraph* (24 November 1991) described Maxwell's style of management as 'crude, brutal and inefficient'. Here was a man who built a great business empire which after his death was shown to be founded on sand. His death left his successors battling to save the empire and ward off the bankers who were persuaded by Maxwell to lend him vast sums of money.

Whilst much may be said about the prudence of the bankers it is significant that Maxwell should have been so persuasive whilst adopting management styles which were not, in Lloyd's view, efficient.

Maxwell was no doubt a man with a high I.Q. and was pr
capable of learning how to lead effectively. It is also likely
even if taught, his personality was such that he would have done
no more than pay lip-service to the use of delegation techniques, to
finding ways of keeping good people or using the brainpower of
his people to the full.

As Lloyd said:

> *Maxwell's public persona appealed to executives*
> *frustrated by lack of excitement in their existing careers*
> *and he could turn on enough charm at first meeting to*
> *persuade them to join. But within three months people*
> *were often looking for a way out . . .*

Lloyd went on in his article to say that Maxwell 'didn't back
people, he bought them and, once bought, they were expected to
be compliant and quiet'.

Could Maxwell have been taught that this was the route to
employing mediocre deadbeats, sycophants and time-servers?
Despite his self-evident cunning the point escaped him.

■ *The truth lies half-way*

Few of us fall into the Nelson category or the Maxwell category.
Most of us are born with an I.Q. around the average, are
moderately sensitive to other people and our environment and can
apply a modicum of common sense to our actions. We can also
improve our leadership capabilities by learning the techniques
which improve effectiveness and by practising them.

The basic requirements

A successful leader must obviously have sufficient technical,
commercial or other knowledge related to his or her particular
field.

Such knowledge, whilst essential, does nothing in itself to
contribute to effective leadership. There are three other broad
attributes which the would-be leader must develop:

 1 The 'right' personal attitudes.

2 The ability to motivate people for whom he or she is responsible.

3 The ability to create and maintain a 'team'.

These requirements demand, in turn, a knowledge of a range of techniques such as:

- How to set objectives and devise plans
- How to train and develop individuals
- Communication, delegation and appraisal.

These skills, which can be taught, will take the would-be leader a great deal further than the basic charm and persuasiveness with which he or she may have been born. Application of these skills will get results.

■ *How does this work out in practice?*

There is a classic life-cycle for every business. Unless changes of direction are made (for example, significant diversification), the business will go through four broad phases from birth to death, as illustrated in the diagram opposite.

Phase 1

This is the period immediately following start-up when market share is low and the business is customer-orientated. The business is likely to be run by an entrepreneur who owns it. He or she will have a small number of employees, possibly none at all initially.

The general atmosphere is likely to be aggressive (in a sales and marketing sense) and creative.

Leadership will be centralised on the founding entrepreneur who will make all decisions of any significance. There will be little delegation but communication will be relatively easy. The small number of people involved means that everyone knows what everyone else is doing and the boss can make his or her wishes known quite effectively on an *ad hoc* basis. The business will be 'informal' and probably innovative.

Phase 2

The business is now established and has moved on from the early

LEADERSHIP STYLES IN THE LIFE-CYCLE OF A BUSINESS

Phase 1	Phase 2	Phase 3	Phase 4
Entrepreneurial	*Developing*	*Established*	*Dying*
Small, customer-orientated with low market share, aggressive and creative.	Growing, market-orientated, strategic and changing.	Formal structures and fixed culture, inert. Bureaucratic and complacent. High market share.	Dominated by crisis and expediency. Mediocrity well established. Sacred cows.
Leadership	*Leadership*	*Leadership*	*Leadership*
Centralised, informal, innovative.	Team-based and innovative.	Formal, within established culture. Resistant to change. Innovation inhibited.	Reactive, exploitative, inconsistent.

Growth

Years

vulnerable phase 1 to a situation in which it is now more strategic, market- as opposed to customer-orientated and changing.

If the entrepreneur has been wise he or she will have delegated some of the decision making and authority and developed a team. Innovation will be frequent as market share increases more rapidly. Some degree of formality will be emerging. The team will work to objectives which will have been jointly agreed and the growing numbers of people will have brought about the need for regular briefing sessions and other fairly formal means of communicating.

Phase 3

The business is now well-established and may be a market leader. A culture will exist which is subject only to minor change and into which all employees must fit.

There will be a great deal of formality such as written 'rules', committees and a hierarchical structure reinforced with status symbols. As an example, possession of a reserved car parking space will be a much treasured and much envied indication of standing within the business.

Innovation will be discouraged by the formality and culture although it is possible that lip service will be paid to it. Change will be slowed down or prevented by a network of committees and bureaucracy. Approval must be obtained for even relatively minor changes and a rigid budgeting structure will effectively block the rapid exploitation of opportunities.

There is likely to be a complacent attitude at senior levels. The size of the company and its market share will create a sense of invulnerability and insufficient regard will be given for competitors' actions and the changes going on in the world at large.

The business will be unexciting and employees with flair and ambition will be discouraged. The culture will promote the retention of mediocre people and risk-taking of any kind will die away. The mediocrity will be self-perpetuating as dull directors and managers will seek non-threatening subordinates of a type similar to themselves.

Phase 4

The years of complacency and inertia will now culminate in the inevitable result. The business will start to die as more thrusting competitors with better products or services erode the market share.

The business could suffer an unwelcome takeover and die a sudden death as its assets are sold off and the remnants absorbed into another business.

The leadership style will reflect the growing awareness of the directors of the threats to the business – and to their personal position and future.

The result is normally an inconsistent approach. Priorities are piled on priorities as a mediocre management reacts to each new blow to the business. 'Task teams' will be formed and abandoned as new ones are created. Blame will be readily apportioned and there will be much running for cover.

The long years of discouragement of change, risk-taking and new thinking will now pay off as a lacklustre management finds that it cannot cope.

Maxwell and the four phases

The history of the Maxwell empire follows this pattern to some extent. The death of the business was as sudden as his own unexpected demise which triggered off the final crisis. However, as the awful facts emerged it became clear that the end was in any case in sight.

The main features of Maxwell's leadership style were:

- He was effective in the phase 1 stage
- His leadership style never changed from the phase 1 type (entrepreneurial and centralised)
- His Rottweiler approach kept everyone in line enabling the business to grow *just as long as his own energy and intelligence could cope with the job of running it.*

Maxwell, like everyone else on this Earth, lacked a monopoly of genius. Had he recognised this, delegated and adopted a participative approach it is likely that the business would have been much better managed. Brains other than his own could have been used to address the problems and opportunities. His own, limited, powers led him to fraudulent acts to keep a seriously ailing business in being and to dupe the outside world into believing all was well.

The business will finally vanish as a result of ineffective leadership.

Not just Maxwell

1991 was a bad year for General Motors. The company, losing money at the rate of 17 million dollars a day in the USA and Canada ended the year by announcing plans to axe the jobs of 74,000 workers and close twenty-one factories. These are signs of a business heading rapidly down the phase 4 slope.

In a report of the company's activities in the *Sunday Times* (22 December 1991) one of the top executives was described as 'an unreconstructed, old-fashioned GM-is-the-best-company-in-the-world type . . . . He has been blocking most of the changes GM needs to make'.

Here we have an example of the effect of the phase 3 complacent attitude which, ironically, mirrors the very attitude adopted by Henry Ford in the 1920s. Ford's unwillingness to vary his hitherto highly successful product enabled General Motors to take over as the world's leading car manufacturers.

Where does effective leadership start?

As mentioned earlier, there are three main attributes which effective leaders must develop: the right personal attitudes; the ability to motivate others; the skills to build and maintain a team.

■ The Right Personal Attitudes

The would-be effective leader starts by taking a good look in the mirror and examining his or her own attitudes.

The 'right' attitudes are the bedrock of being able to lead well – and consistently well – at all levels of management and in any field of activity. The reflection in the mirror should show:

- An awareness (put into practice) that people matter and that the effective leader takes people with him or her.

- An understanding of the many human characteristics which can inhibit progress and how the resulting obstacles can be overcome.

- A willingness to look for and size up the facts – avoiding shooting from the hip. This demands the personal discipline to eschew the easy option of taking off-the-cuff decisions in favour of judgement based on 'research' and analysis.

- Readiness to make changes. Without change, which can sometimes be painful, progress is impossible. The effective leader suppresses his or her own natural reluctance to accept change and will actually initiate it. Then the effective leader will follow it through with persistence and patience, accompanied by a willingness to adapt or alter the direction or nature of the change until a successful result is achieved.

- Willingness to learn. No matter how experienced or well-qualified a leader may be there is always more to learn. The world changes and new ideas emerge. These new ideas – which can sometimes be learned from subordinates – are ignored at the leader's peril.

- Enthusiasm for the training and development of subordinates. The effective leader will encourage learning in his or her people and create opportunities for them to gain knowledge and skills.

- A preference for working in a systematic and ordered way. Disciplined activity will be preferred to chaos and *ad hoc* actions.

- Ability to set objectives and devise plans to meet them – as opposed to working day to day on an expediency basis. This requires the discipline to recognise and distinguish between what is urgent and what is important and then to set priorities.

- Readiness to face problems and deal with them –

avoiding the temptation to find the excuse to do something else in the hope that the problems will go away.

- Willingness to give up 'technical work' which he or she may be good at and enjoy in favour of managing the human resources, that is, leading the people.

- Acceptance that learning and using management techniques appropriate to his or her job will be more successful than an instinctive approach.

All very theoretical? Sounds good but not relevant to you? Try this self-check questionnaire. You need not show the answers to anyone else so you can be brutally honest!

Personal Attitudes – Self-Check Questionnaire

	YES	NO
1 I set aside planned time for talking with the people I am responsible for – and do it.	☐	☐
2 Before taking any significant decision I always consult the people who will be affected.	☐	☐
3 I listen patiently and sympathetically to any of my staff who has a problem and I give support.	☐	☐
4 I always obtain the facts before taking a decision – even if the fact-finding is something of a bore.	☐	☐
5 I suppress my natural instinct to oppose new ideas and always give them proper consideration.	☐	☐
6 My staff regularly come to me with new ideas.	☐	☐
7 There is a history of successful change which I can point to in my area of responsibility.	☐	☐

8 I have a regular programme of self-development. For example, learning new skills or technology and can list my learning achievements over the past two years.

☐ ☐

9 There is a written development and training plan for all the people who report to me. They are all aware of it and I monitor progress regularly.

☐ ☐

10 The work in my area is carried out in a systematic way. The systems are reviewed at regular intervals with the people concerned.

☐ ☐

11 Both I and my subordinates have clear objectives and plans to achieve them. Objectives and plans are reviewed regularly.

☐ ☐

12 *All* my people know what my personal objectives are and the reason for them.

☐ ☐

13 *All* objectives and plans have been put together with the involvement of the people affected.

☐ ☐

14 I never brush aside problems, dump them on someone else or just ignore them.

☐ ☐

15 At least 50 per cent of my time is spent on managing my team rather than technical work.

☐ ☐

16 I have learned and evaluated management techniques such as appraisal, delegation, objective setting and analytical methods and apply them when appropriate.

☐ ☐

Now add up the number of ticks in the 'YES' boxes.

If you have scored sixteen out of sixteen you are either kidding yourself or you are the world's most balanced leader.

Anything over twelve is a very good score but clearly there is room for improvement.

A score of less than eight suggests that you have a long way to go.

Having done this self-check you can now repeat the process in respect to *your boss*. How does he or she match up? The chances are that you will find much to criticise – and that is likely to reflect how your subordinates also see you! Few of us can afford to be complacent.

■ *Motivating the people*

The ability to motivate the people is the second of the required attributes of the effective leader. This is a lengthy subject dealt with in full in the next chapter. The ways and means to shift people from being contented but fairly passive workers to ones with enthusiasm and energy are many and varied. Motivational skills can be taught and normally need to be. Despite the fact that all of us respond in much the same way to motivating factors (and demotivating ones), very few people identify and use the motivators in anything more than a random way.

The leader who is conscious of what actions motivate people and how he or she can bring them into play will be more effective. Avoiding the demotivators is equally important, particularly since these are often subtle in nature and only too easy to employ without realising it. Consider just one real-life example:

Hannah and the new broom

Hannah (not her real name) was promoted. She took over the management of a division of her company which included a number of clerical departments and a computer department. Anxious to make an impression, Hannah declared that punctuality had to improve and *without consulting the heads of department* issued an edict that all staff would in future have to 'sign in' on arrival at work in the morning. Hannah would then personally interview any latecomers and anyone without an acceptable excuse (not defined) would be for the high jump. The new rule was made known to staff by means of a coldly worded notice on the bulletin board.

The head of the computer department protested to Hannah, pointing out that his staff worked overtime (unpaid), were obliged by the nature of their work to work odd hours and could be called from their beds if something went wrong on the night shift. Hannah heard the objections but insisted that there could be no exceptions as 'fairness' demanded that all staff should be treated equally. The result was a refusal on the part of the computer staff to work late, at night or on weekends. As one of them put it, 'No one can expect me to sit here until 11.00 at night and then have to explain why I am five minutes late the next morning.'

Hannah realised she was on a loser and quickly dropped the idea by allowing it to slide into disuse.'

What did Hannah do wrong?

Hannah's fundamental error was to take action (action which would affect *all* the staff) without consulting her heads of department. If she had done so she would at least have heard the computer manager's views and given herself a chance to avoid damaging the goodwill on which the computer department depended.

Her second mistake was to put a notice on the board. Having done this there was no possible retreat.

Her third mistake was to allow her time-checking scheme to die away. She could have saved the situation by *publicly* admitting that she had made a mistake and cancelling the whole scheme. This would have required courage but would have gained her some much needed respect.

'OK,' I hear you say, 'but how many people would be so silly? The situation only required a bit of common sense.'

You would be right about the common sense but good leadership needs a little more. Remember that Hannah was a real-life person with lengthy management experience. Her colleagues thought she had plenty of common sense. What she had never had was formal training in leadership. If she had, she would have learned the rule 'always consult before acting'.

A cautionary note

A golden rule which Hannah also failed to observe was, 'Never try to sweep like a new broom.' Anyone newly appointed to leadership of an established unit should avoid rushing in with changes. The people in the unit will be suspicious of a new leader and time is needed to establish a trusting relationship. The new leader will also need time to find out how things work, who are the dominant people in the group, why things are done in a particular way and so on. Things are not always what they seem at first sight and time is needed to obtain the facts. This is reflected in the third of the right personal attitudes required of an effective leader listed earlier (see page 21), a willingness to look for and size up the facts.

■ Building and maintaining a team

People do not work together as a team by accident or as a natural consequence of being together. In fact the opposite often happens as rivalries, jealousies and conflicting ambitions take hold. Teams have to be built and maintained. The effective leader needs to know how to do this, starting with a basic understanding of what a team actually is and knowing how to recognise whether it exists or not.

Team building (covered in detail in chapter 3) is an essential prerequisite to efficient working and profit.

Summary of Main Points

1 Leadership cannot be defined in a few words but, paradoxically, it is entirely possible to identify what is needed for effective leadership.

2 There are no born leaders but there are people born with characteristics which are conducive to effective leadership.

3 The skills and techniques required to be an effective leader can be taught but there are some people whose characteristics are such that learning them will make little difference.

4 The basic requirements for effective leadership are:

- Definable personal attitudes
- The ability to motivate people
- The ability to create and maintain a team.

These requirements demand, in turn, a knowledge and understanding of a range of techniques.

5 The 'classic' life-cycle of a business from birth to death reflects leadership effectiveness (or lack of it) and can indicate what must be done to keep a business prospering.

6 Your own (and perhaps your boss's) attitudes can be checked using the questionnaire in this chapter.

7 Motivating the people means shifting them from being merely contented (or actually demotivated) to applying energy and enthusiasm to their jobs. This requires the conscious awareness in the leader of the ways and means to do it.

8 Team building also requires specific skills which we are not born with. People will not necessarily work in a co-operative, co-ordinated and naturally supportive way without the right leadership.

2 Should We Believe the Gurus?

Since the Second World War and particularly in the 1960s and 1970s a number of management gurus emerged.to tell us how to lead and motivate the people who work for us. For some years it seemed that as soon as we had taken on board the latest fashionable theory another one was presented to us. It is not surprising that many managers have adopted a cynical attitude to some of the views put forward – especially since some of the gurus have been seen to make vast sums of money by offering seminars on their ideas at upmarket conference centres.

The jargon used by some experts has also given rise to doubts. Pseudo-scientific language which no one is likely to use in everyday life does nothing to make an idea more understandable.

This is a pity because much of the work done by behavioural scientists has resulted in ideas which, when applied with a dose of common sense, have considerable potential value for leaders.

It is also sad that much of the advice given by the better thinkers is dismissed as being obvious. There are many things in life which are obvious – *once they have been pointed out*! Until that happens, the obvious is often ignored and not acted upon. This at least explains why some fundamental mistakes are made by less than effective leaders in situations where the adverse result was 'obvious'.

So, the sayings of the gurus are worth looking at and seeing how to convert their ideas into practical applications. Doing so satisfies another of the attitude requirements mentioned earlier (page 21):

that the effective manager is willing to learn and will, no matter how experienced, examine ideas which are new to him or her.

This chapter examines the ideas of three (out of many) of the gurus, Hertzberg, Maslow and Likert. These three developed their ideas in the late 1950s and early 1960s and you may ask why more recent researchers are not included. The reason is that Hertzberg, Maslow and Likert between them identified all the essential factors in leading and motivating. Their ideas have passed the test of time and the many useful and interesting offerings of more recently published gurus have not brought about any fundamental changes in leadership thinking. This should not be a surprise since human nature is unlikely to have changed over the last thirty to forty years!

Frederick Hertzberg

Hertzberg, an American researcher into the 'psychology of work', put forward the so-called Hygiene-Motivation theory. Don't let this piece of jargon put you off – underneath it is some good stuff.

The hygiene factors

According to Hertzberg there are a number of factors (which you the leader can influence) which will have a demotivating effect on your people. They are all concerned with the administrative and environmental aspects of the jobs of your people. These Hertzberg called hygiene factors, perhaps because they are akin to health hazards. Get them wrong and things will go wrong. Getting them right means normality will return.

It is obvious that if you are late in paying the wages you will have trouble on your hands. You may avoid a wholesale walk-out but you are likely to have some very fed-up and unenthusiastic people to deal with. What is far less obvious is that similar adverse reactions can be caused by lesser failures such as:

- Unreliable vending machines
- Dirty offices
- Poor food in the canteen
- Photocopiers which break down

- Unresolved conflict. For example, who is responsible for the filing?
- Rules which are perceived as being petty or pointless
- Adverse effect of work on home life
- Weak supervision
- Real or apparent favouritism

Failures in any such areas will demotivate your people. Correcting the situation will not make them positively motivated (we will look at motivation later) but will at least restore them to a 'contented' state.

A real-life moan

A number of secretaries in a generally lacklustre department were interviewed by the author to find out why morale was low. These are their comments:

1 The printers on our personal computers have been provided with paper which seems to be of the wrong weight. The result is that we waste a lot of time with paper creasing and crashing in the printer rollers.

2 The photocopier repeatedly breaks down and causes delays.

3 The label printer breaks down several times a day and we waste a lot of time, delay completion of mail, and destroy an enormous number of labels.

4 Our bosses frequently disappear without telling us where they are going or when. This looks extremely bad when customers ring in and we are unable to give them any sensible information.

5 The quality of dictation is extremely poor and sometimes urgent telexes are mixed with non-urgent letters on the same tape. This causes considerable aggravation and delay.

6 The fax machine is set up so that the identification information has to appear on every single page. This means that where we have a fax involving several

pages we waste a great deal of time having to reformat what should be an automatic computer function to get rid of this identification. If we allow the identification to go through it will appear on every page of the fax and apart from wasting money it looks silly.

7 The system for hashing on and camping on the telephones does not work properly and so calls often go to the wrong extension.

8 Executives have a habit of demanding that they be given the file for each item of post even when the file is not necessary to deal with that item of post. The result is a great deal of pulling of files and putting them back in the racks afterwards. It also clogs up the executive's desk with files he or she often does not need.

9 Temporary files are often made up when the original file has gone missing. There is a tendency to make up temporary files without seriously looking for the original and so there is then a danger of duplication and paper not being in its proper place.

It is interesting to note that it was the general environment which was upsetting the secretaries. They were not unhappy about the *content* of their jobs. It was the *context* which bothered them.

It was also significant that:

- Some of their bosses were unaware of the problems
- One said he was aware but it was not his job to do anything about it
- Some were aware but regarded the grumbles as petty

The last point is particularly interesting in that it illustrates the point that the 'obvious' is not always recognised and that something which is petty to one person can be very important to someone else.

This is one of Hertzberg's points. The 'petty' matters matter. The effective leader will always make time to see that the environmental factors in the job are as good as they ought to be and not a constant irritant which erodes enthusiasm.

■ The motivating factors

In addition to the hygiene factors, which can demotivate if neglected, Hertzberg pointed to a range of motivators. He divided these into short- and long-term influences on the individual worker.

The short-term factors are:

- A sense of achievement
- Recognition

The long-term factors are:

- Amount of responsibility
- Prospects of advancement
- Interesting work
- 'Growth' possibilities

Let us examine these factors, starting with the short-term ones.

A sense of achievement

A junior supervisor working in a shop belonging to a retail chain came home one night and told her husband that her section had not only achieved their sales target but had done better than any other section. Following this achievement she voluntarily started to go in early each day to see that everything was properly set up for the day's trading. That was motivation resulting from a sense of achievement. Without prompting, her team of people also began to put in a little extra to the job – they too had derived a sense of achievement.

Most, if not all of us, know from personal experience that achieving something stimulates us to make further efforts. It is certainly true that failure has the opposite, depressing effect.

However, a sense of achievement will not necessarily come about just as a result of a job well done. The effective leader must help to create it.

In our case of the shop supervisor someone had set a target which had given her something to aim for. She was also given a means to measure her results against the target and to know that she had achieved something. Providing a benchmark and a way to measure results against it is the job of the leader. Exhortations simply to work harder or to 'improve productivity' will not have the same effect.

Recognition

This goes hand in glove with the sense of achievement. Public recognition is more effective than private recognition but any form of pat on the back has a good effect.

It costs nothing for the leader to make a suitable comment:

> *'Thanks for getting those invoices out, George.'*
> *'You did a good job there, Susie.'*
> *'Congratulations on your exam results.'*
> *'That was a good order you brought in yesterday.'*

The effect of such recognition can be quite dramatic but the achievement in itself need not be. Recognition of even a small success is worth a lot in terms of motivation.

But it's only short-term

Motivation from a sense of achievement and/or recognition has, Hertzberg found, only a short-term effect. It wears off and must be repeated from time to time. The effective leader will therefore seek ways and means to provide the reinforcement.

Now let's look at the long-term factors.

Amount of responsibility

It is not unknown for managers to declare that the average person (whoever that may be) does not want responsibility and will go to some trouble to avoid it. Observation and the findings of many of the gurus shows that in many, perhaps most, cases this is not true. The fact is that given responsibility the majority of people are stimulated by it and rise to the occasion. Naturally, authority must go with the responsibility if it is to be a benefit rather than a burden. However, this authority need not include power over other people. All that is needed is the delegated power to make decisions on how to do the job without having to refer upstream for every jot and tittle about what to do, when and how.

The essential requirement is to ensure that employees are aware of what is expected of them, the resources at their disposal and the extent of authority being delegated.

Hertzberg found that giving a responsibility did have a motivating effect and, even if he or she has some misgivings, the would-be effective leader will try it out. Successes are likely to be more common than failures and the latter are more often the result of poor delegation.

Prospects of advancement

There is nothing more stultifying than the perception that any form of advancement is limited or absent altogether. This is often a problem in family-owned businesses where it is clear that the plum jobs are reserved for family members. The same occurs in certain partnerships made up of people with a similar background.

The converse is also true. Hertzberg found that a clear prospect of rising to higher things would motivate the people who wanted to go further. It should be noted that it is the *prospect* of advancement that is the motivator – not necessarily a cast-iron guarantee of a place on the board. Family firms will need to think about this question very carefully. If the policy is to restrict top-level jobs to family members then any really able and ambitious employees will be discouraged. The long-term future of the business may be better served by a policy which makes a positive provision for 'outsiders' to be given senior (including board) positions. This also improves the chance of maintaining a high level of I.Q. and ability at the top where it is needed. Families do not necessarily have a monopoly of genius. Any policy for giving top jobs to non-family people must be made public – and seen to be acted upon when circumstances permit. Remember, it is the prospect which counts but the prospect must be one which employees can believe in.

Interesting work

This looks like a tricky one since what may be interesting to one person may not be interesting to another. We need to identify the features of work which make it interesting. You can do this for yourself easily enough by examining your own experience and listing the attributes of work which interested you in the past. Most people's list includes some or all of the following:

- An element of variety
- Difficult enough to offer challenges (but not so difficult as to cause stress)
- Meeting and being involved with other people
- A dynamic environment, for example, where innovation is a feature of the organisation
- Freedom to initiate or make changes
- Knowing what it is all for, what the end-product is and why things are done in a particular way
- Having a part in making decisions – especially setting objectives and the plans to achieve them

Some of these attributes of interesting work were pointed out by other gurus, in particular by Rensis Likert whose work will be discussed later in this chapter. The effective leader will recognise the needs of each individual and make positive efforts to make every job as interesting as possible, however difficult that may seem to be. It is not always feasible to make every job a matter of excited fascination but ways can nearly always be found to raise it from the level of humdrum routine.

A pressing point of interest
An intelligent student took a temporary job in a factory to supplement his meagre grant. He was given the job of operating a machine which made parts for electrical machinery by pressing raw plastic into a mould. The work was hot, dirty, tiring and above all highly repetitive. The mould was opened, the plastic poured in, the mould was closed, a handle pulled and the pressing made. The mould was opened, the pressing removed and the whole dreary cycle started again. The student could have been forgiven for giving up or going mad. In fact he found the job remarkably interesting.

Why? Because the boss gave him something to think about. The manager of the department, having allowed the student a day or two to learn the job, suggested that he might like to experiment a little with it. He could try, for example, preparing a number of 'shots' of plastic first and then doing a run on the machine. He could compare this with preparing each shot of plastic and using it before preparing the next. This and similar options were given, provided that output and quality did not fall below standards laid down.

For a few days the student was busy (and interested) trying different ideas until he had worked out what he considered was the best system. He then reported back to his boss.

The boss was smart enough to recognise the student's achievement (using one of Hertzberg's short-term motivators), and then said, 'OK, it's your machine, do the job in the way you think best.' The student, with this freedom, found the job interesting for the duration of a three-month stint – and went back again to do it all again in the following year.

Are they all like that?

You may say that an intelligent student is not typical of the people on the shop floor. 'What about the others?' you may ask. 'Most of them are not bright enough to be trusted to try out experiments.'

This may be true in a *very few* cases. It is arguable that the average I.Q. on the shop floor is no lower than that in the boardroom. Unless you as a manager are positive that you can learn nothing from your people (however lowly) then give them the chance to think. They will gain an interest in the job and you will gain improved productivity.

Possibility of growth

Here we have a piece of real old guru's jargon. What on earth do they mean by growth? Hertzberg was referring to opportunity to work outside a restricted and narrow job description.

The individual, he pointed out, needs to see wider horizons. This can be achieved by:

- Training and development schemes
- Transfers to gain experience

- Exposure to pressure, problems and opportunities additional to the usual ones, for example, by membership of a project team
- Working, perhaps temporarily, alongside a specialist to gain new skills or at least an appreciation of them.

The growth opportunities provided need not, indeed sometimes cannot, be great or dramatic. Membership of a committee may be enough.

Must we provide them all – all the time?

It is not reasonable or often possible to suppose that any employee can be kept in a permanent state of high motivation. However, it is possible to provide *some* of the motivating conditions which Hertzberg recommends from time to time, maybe even most of the time. The leader's job is to consider his or her people as individuals, estimate their needs and provide as many of the motivating factors as is practical.

■ Money – the $64,000 question

Does money motivate? Hertzberg placed money in both lists: as a hygiene factor *and* as a motivator.

There is no doubt that money is a hygiene factor, if you don't get enough a great depression falls upon you. But how much is enough?

If income is too low to sustain a reasonable or adequate standard of living, as judged by the individual, then it will not be enough. It will also be considered too little if the individual believes his or her salary is lower than that of colleagues doing the same job. It is not necessary for this to be true, only for the individual to believe it is true. It is an unfortunate fact of life that most people will readily suspect that colleagues are being paid more. It is also a fact that an employee will work well and be content (if other factors are adequate) until the suspicion of inequality is born. When that happens the hitherto acceptable salary becomes unacceptable and the employee loses enthusiasm.

It is not surprising that in those cases where women are paid less than men doing the same job (and everyone knows it), that the productivity of the women is sometimes lower. This is then used as the excuse for paying them less!

'Women make less effort than men so why should they be paid as much?' asked one manager at a seminar on motivation. The question which should have been asked was, 'Some *employees* make less effort than others – can we identify the reasons why and do something about it?'

So, inadequate income will demotivate but does an increase in salary motivate? Almost certainly yes – but only for a time. Think back to your own last salary increase. It is a pound to a penny that your thoughts followed the following sequence:

1 You were pleased to receive your increase especially if it was a generous one. You had a feeling that your efforts were appreciated.

2 Your level of motivation was raised and you went about your work with more 'zip'.

3 Time went by and you became used to the larger pay cheque. Your mind began to contemplate a higher salary still. (The initial 'zip' is wearing off rapidly.)

4 The next salary review date approached and you began to speculate on what you might get. Various (and probably increasing) figures passed through your thoughts.

5 You finally fixed on the new, higher figure that you thought you should get. Your actual salary by comparison now looked positively niggardly – and you felt undervalued. Your motivation level sank and you became less than content with your lot.

Salary is therefore one of the motivators but only in the short term. There is, however, another important aspect of salary: it can reflect status.

Status and money

Most individuals are concerned about their standing in their work and social communities. The existence of status symbols in the workplace is a reflection of this, as is the effort which people will make to acquire them. Car parking spaces, personal assistants, first-class travel and a more expensive company car are all examples of the status symbols which are fought for with relentless determination in some organisations.

Salary can also be a prime status symbol. This was amply illustrated in the United Kingdom in the 1970s when the marginal rate of income tax was around 98 per cent. Despite the fact that the tax man would take almost all of any addition to salary, putative leaders of nationalised industries demanded higher salaries to take the job. The only rational explanation is that the size of the salary represented status. Status-conscious bosses felt it vital that their salaries were at least comparable with those of the big bosses of private industry, even if their spendable income was scarcely affected.

On the payroll – but on the team?

It is sometimes said that the only consistent value of a very high salary is to keep an employee on the payroll. However, this does not mean that employees will be motivated. Their presence can be bought but their enthusiasm must be earned in other ways.

■ Hertzberg's ideas in summary

Summarising what may be learned from Hertzberg we find that:

1 The effective leader must ensure that administrative matters, the working environment and salary must be satisfactory to employees if they are not to become demotivated.

Making them satisfactory will not motivate in itself but will remove negative effects.

2 Short-term measures to motivate include:

- Providing the employee with a sense of achievement
- Giving recognition for good work.

3 Long-term motivation can be achieved by:

- Giving responsibility
- Providing visible opportunity for future advancement
- Adding interest to the work
- Providing 'growth' possibilities.

Anyone wishing to delve more deeply into Hertzberg's work should look in second-hand bookshops for a copy of his *Work and the Nature of Man* (Staples Press, 1968) or *The Motivation to Work* by F. Hertzberg, B. Mausner and B.B. Snyderman (Wiley, 1959).

Abraham Maslow

■ *Maslow's Hierarchy of Needs*

Maslow, an American psychologist, came up with a theory known as the 'Hierarchy of Needs'. This is another piece of jargon which need not put you off as the concept itself is quite straight-forward.

Maslow argued in *Toward a Psychology of Being* (Van Nostrand Reinhold, 1968) that people *motivate themselves* as a result of a desire to satisfy various needs.

At the most basic level we all have physiological needs such as food, drink and sleep. According to Maslow, anyone lacking these basic essentials will be motivated to satisfy them and will not need encouragement from anyone else. This simple view is probably one which all of us will go along with as it involves survival itself. In extreme cases, people have risked their lives to obtain food and even killed for it.

Close behind the basic needs comes 'security'. The starving man having found some food will probably turn next to consideration of his own safety and shelter.

Today's manager is not likely to be faced with employees motivated by these very basic needs. The employees' salaries will provide the wherewithal to shop at the local supermarket and pay the rent or mortgage.

We should as leaders look at what Maslow defines as the higher needs, ones he believes influence the behaviour of our people at work. Maslow divides them into three groups:

Social needs   –   Sense of belonging

                        Social activity

                        Affection (love)

Self-esteem needs – Self-respect

Status

Esteem of others

Self-fulfilment needs – Growth

Personal development

Accomplishment

Creativity.

Maslow holds that if social and self-esteem needs are not met the employee will exhibit one or more of:

- Aggression
- Non-co-operation
- Apathy
- Alienation.

If these needs are met but self-fulfilment is not the employee will exhibit:

- Satisfaction with the job
- Passive contentment.

If all three needs are met, Maslow says the employee will exhibit:

- Work motivation
- A creative interest in the work.

Later researchers have pointed out that a lack of opportunity to satisfy some of the higher needs can lead to stress and ill-health. This result can be observed both on the shop floor and in the boardroom, along with a distinct lack of motivation.

Keeping the drive going

One of the most important features of Maslow's theory is that once a need is satisfied it is no longer a motivator and the worker must have the opportunity to strive to satisfy a higher need if he or she is to continue to be anything more than passive.

■ The practical application of Maslow's ideas

Managers might be forgiven for treating Maslow's ideas as interesting theory and nothing more but, like Hertzberg's findings, they clearly point to actions which the leader can take to become more effective.

Let's look at some of the needs which Maslow listed and put them into real-life job contexts.

A sense of belonging

This need points to the importance of a professional approach to the induction of new employees. This skill goes far beyond a handshake and telling the newcomer that his or her desk is in the corner next to the door. Induction is a key factor in making people feel part of the operation. Poor induction can (and often does) result in demotivation and an early resignation.

Social activity and affection

We do not have to go dancing with our employees every night or repeatedly tell them how much we like them. We should, however, create opportunities for our people to share some time in a 'social' way even if this is only by provision of a place where they can eat their lunchtime sandwiches together. This, combined with the promotion of a friendly and relaxed atmosphere, will enable people to feel part of a group and not merely an individual among many.

Self-respect, status and the esteem of others

These can be enhanced by applying the right communication techniques. Action can be as simple as adopting a courteous and respectful attitude when talking to an employee. There is an old saying that 'respect commands respect'. Respect also encourages self-respect. The same courtesy (including, for example, patient listening to a junior) enhances a sense of status. It is not necessary to give someone a fancy title as a status symbol to show that he or she is valued.

Praise when due and support for an employee experiencing difficulties will also help. Failure to praise and destructive complaining will reduce the self-esteem and status of the employee.

Self-fulfilment needs
These are often regarded as the most difficult to meet but this view is not valid.

A personal development plan should exist for *each* of your people. The plan need not be complicated or necessarily look ahead for many years but it should be there.

Training and the opportunity for wider experience will be the basis of the plan and will benefit you as leader by virtue of having a more capable member of your team.

Accomplishment and creativity needs can be met by providing, through delegation, the opportunity for the employee to do something in his or her way.

How does Maslow match up to Hertzberg?

There is much similarity between the two theories even if expressed in very different ways. Both talk about growth and achievement (accomplishment). Both mention status (recognition) and both refer to working relationships (social activity).

Above all, both indicate a similar range of actions which the leader must take to improve effectiveness. The nuts and bolts of these actions are dealt with in later chapters when we look at the hands-on techniques of the effective leader.

Rensis Likert

One of the less well-known gurus, Likert (Director, Institute for Social Research, University of Michigan) has some very sound stuff to offer. Having studied a range of leaders and their way of going about things, Likert divided their styles into four types which he called 'systems'. They can be summarised as follows:

■ Likert's Four Systems

1 THE EXPLOITATIVE-AUTHORITATIVE SYSTEM in which decisions are imposed on subordinates, where threats are used to 'motivate', where high levels of management have much responsibility but lower levels have virtually none, where there is little communication and no teamwork.

2 THE BENEVOLENT-AUTHORITATIVE SYSTEM in which leadership amounts to a condescending form of master–servant relationship. Motivation is mainly by rewards, managerial personnel feel responsibility but lower levels do not, there is little communication and relatively little teamwork.

3 THE CONSULTATIVE SYSTEM in which leadership is by superiors who have substantial but not complete trust in their subordinates. Motivation is by rewards and some involvement. A high proportion of personnel, but more especially those at the higher levels, feel responsible for achieving organisational goals. There is some communication (both vertical and horizontal) and a moderate amount of teamwork.

4 THE PARTICIPATIVE-GROUP SYSTEM in which leadership is by superiors who have complete confidence in their subordinates, motivation is by economic rewards based on goals which have been set in participation, personnel at all levels feel real responsibility for the organisational goals, there is much communication, and a substantial amount of co-operative teamwork.

Likert stated that system 4 yields the best results and system 1 the worst. He based this view on observation and measurement in real-life cases particularly in sales team leadership. In his book *The Human Organisation* (McGraw-Hill, 1967, reproduced by permission of McGraw-Hill), he includes the following diagram which illustrates the situation that he found.

Likert's findings also indicate the characteristics of the successful team and the unsuccessful. They can be summarised as follows.

Unsuccessful	Successful
1 Staff inhibited in discussing work with superior.	No fears or inhibitions.
2 Boss does not obtain subordinates' ideas in problem solving.	Frequent involvement of staff.
3 Staff 'motivated' by fear, threats, punishment.	Motivation by rewards linked to the achievement of agreed objectives.

LIKERT'S SYSTEMS COMPARED AS APPLIED TO SALES MANAGEMENT

**If a manager has:
a well-organised plan of operation,
high-performance goals,
technical competence**

and if the manager manages via:

Systems 1 or 2	System 4
e.g., uses direct hierarchical pressure for results, including the usual contests and other practices of the traditional systems	e.g., uses the principle of supportive relationships, group methods of supervision, and other features of System 4

his organisation will display:

less group loyalty	greater group loyalty
lower performance goals	higher performance goals
greater conflict and less co-operation	greater co-operation
less technical assistance to peers	more technical assistance to peers
greater feeling of unreasonable pressure	less feeling of unreasonable pressure
less favourable attitudes towards manager	more favourable attitudes towards manager
lower motivation to produce	higher motivation to produce

and his organisation will attain:

lower sales volume	higher sales volume
higher sales costs	lower sales costs
lower quality of business sold	higher quality of business sold

Unsuccessful	Successful
4 Only senior staff feel responsible for achieving organisation's goals. (Juniors often hostile.)	All staff feel responsible.
5 Very little communication with subordinates regarding the goals to be achieved, why or how.	Continuous communication and explanation with individuals.
6 Information flow is mainly downwards.	Information flows freely in all directions.
7 Information received by subordinates is viewed with suspicion.	Information accepted and often openly discussed.
8 Any upwards flow of information tends to be inaccurate – what the boss wants to hear and often carefully selected.	Upwards flow of information is free, accurate, complete and honest.
9 Little knowledge of subordinates' problems.	Problems known and understood.
10 Absence of co-operative teamwork. Staff work as individuals.	Substantial teamwork and problems shared.
11 Bulk of decisions are made at the top.	Decision making is widely spread and co-ordinated via an overlapping group.
12 Decision makers are largely unaware of lower-level problems.	There is substantial awareness and appreciation of lower-level problems.
13 Staff are little involved in decisions about their work.	Staff are consulted and often involved in decision taking.
14 Goals are set by issuing orders.	Goals are agreed by group discussion. Orders given after full discussion.

15 Control is exercised from the top only.	Control is delegated to all levels. Some activities controlled mostly at lower levels.
16 There is an informal organisation which opposes management.	Informal and formal are the same, there is no 'underground' leadership structure.
17 Performance results are used to police and punish.	Results are used for self-guidance. Not punitive.

We are, with Likert, getting closer to the action which the leader must take to be effective and you can see that his ideas are compatible with those of Hertzberg.

The prize for the leader who takes these ideas on board was well-expressed by Likert who offered this view on motivated people:

> *The motivation of the members of an organisation can be crucial in determining whether labour-saving processes – computers or automated equipment – are made to work well or poorly. Supervisory and non-supervisory employees, if they wish to do so, can make excellent equipment perform unsatisfactorily and with frequent failures. These employees can also, if they desire to do so, rapidly eliminate the inadequacies in new processes or equipment and have the operation running smoothly in a surprisingly short time.*

This is an interesting point which will ring a bell with systems analysts and others with the experience (sometimes painful) of getting new computer systems and other innovations off the ground. If the people are enthusiastic it will work. If they are not, it won't, even if the system is a good one.

What does it all add up to?

If we combine the findings of the three gurus we begin to see, in broad terms, what the effective leader must do.

1 Provide challenge and the opportunity for fulfilment:

- By setting objectives jointly agreed with employees and ensuring that they are properly inducted
- By encouraging employees to put forward ideas and

wherever possible to allow the same employees to develop and implement them

- By allowing employees to 'run their own show'.

2 Provide for individual development:

- By training the people – on and off the job
- By allocating work to make fullest use of individual skills
- By giving support in weak areas.

3 Recognise achievement:

- By reporting regularly on achievements
- By giving praise where due.

4 Make each individual feel valued:

- By involving them in decision making, for example, by seeking their opinion and listening to it
- By monitoring their work, discussing it with them and being aware of their problems
- By making clear to them the importance of what they do and how it fits in to the general scheme.

5 To develop team working, the subject of the next chapter.

SUMMARY OF MAIN POINTS

1 The effective leader, undeterred by the jargon used, will find much useful guidance from some of the management gurus.

2 The work of Hertzberg, Maslow and Likert is worthy of close attention and can be translated into practical action which leaders can take to improve their performance.

3 Hertzberg described the factors which will demotivate. He also described the attributes of work which will positively motivate the worker.

4 Hertzberg's motivating factors include:

- Sense of achievement

- Recognition
- Amount of responsibility
- Prospects for advancement
- Interesting work
- Growth possibilities.

The message for leaders is that they must provide at least one or two of these motivators for at least some of the time. It can be done.

5 Money will motivate only in a limited way. Man does not live by bread alone and although you may buy his presence you cannot buy his enthusiasm.

6 Maslow pointed out that people have needs and motivation (which comes from within) is based on meeting these needs.

7 Maslow's definition of the needs is compatible with Hertzberg's views and further indicates what the leader must do to be effective.

8 Maslow points to the importance of well-constructed induction schemes, social opportunities, communication and good old-fashioned courtesy. At the top of the scale are finding ways to satisfy self-fulfilment needs by providing team members with challenge and opportunity.

9 Likert identified four 'systems' of leadership ranging from the Exploitative/Authoritative approach to the Participative/Group style. He found the latter worked best in practice.

10 The gurus point to a strategy for effective leadership which involves:

- Clear objectives – understood and agreed by the people
- Employee involvement in control and decision making
- Development of the people
- Giving the opportunity to achieve – and recognising it when it happens
- Enhancing a sense of belonging in a team, having status and value and seeing a future which appeals.

3 Building the Team

You may already be leading a team (or be a member of one) rather than just a collection of individuals. However, are you sure that you really do have a team? Try the following check.

	YES	NO
1 Do you believe that for at least 90 per cent of the time all of your people are pulling their weight?	☐	☐
2 Are they all pulling in the same direction, i.e., you do not have to sort out conflicts over what should be done and how?	☐	☐
3 Does every one of your people find it possible to obtain support from colleagues when they need it?	☐	☐
4 If there is a 'crisis' can you depend on everyone willingly pitching in to sort it out?	☐	☐
5 When something goes wrong is *everyone* concerned about it?	☐	☐
6 Do your people find and express pleasure in the success of colleagues?	☐	☐

7 Do your people depend on each other to do what they promise to do? ☐ ☐

8 Does everyone in your team feel that they belong? ☐ ☐

9 Does everyone feel that he or she matters? ☐ ☐

10 Do your people readily report problems and failures – fully and frankly? ☐ ☐

11 Do your people voluntarily pick up work which has been overlooked or neglected even if it is someone else's responsibility? ☐ ☐

12 Are people missed when they are away, for example, are they warmly greeted on return? ☐ ☐

13 Do your people have a clear idea of what the objectives are both for individuals and the team as a whole? ☐ ☐

14 Does everyone have a clear idea of who does what, when and why? ☐ ☐

15 Do your people ask each other for advice and get it? ☐ ☐

How do you score? Yes, you! It is the leader being tested not the team.

If you scored fifteen 'Yes' answers you are probably being less critical than you should be. Being that good is nearly impossible.

Any score of ten or over shows that things are on the right track but five or below indicates that there is a lot to remedy.

If you were unable to answer any of the questions because you didn't know you could have a serious problem on your hands. You could be working in an ivory tower and need to get much closer to the action. No one ever led a successful team from behind a permanently closed door – unless there was a very loyal deputy to do it instead.

The characteristics of a team

The questions have already given you a picture of what features make a team. They can be summarised into six criteria.

- *A definable membership.*
  It is clear who belongs to the team and no one is left on the periphery of an 'in-group'.

- *A shared sense of purpose.*
  Everyone knows what has to be done and why – and has had a hand in deciding these things.

- *Group pride.*
  There is a distinct *ésprit de corps*. People are proud of their presence and part in the group and may even boast about it to others.

- *A clearly visible interdependence.*
  Members of the group support each other willingly and there is a shared sense that everyone must succeed for the group to be successful.

- *Much interaction between the members.*
  There are no pockets of solitary workers doing their own thing whether by choice or otherwise.

- *The group works as a single organism.*

- *Members want the team to succeed.*
  They will put this above personal ambition.

How is this Utopia achieved?

Teams do not appear automatically when a group of people are put together. The leader must *create* the team from the people and then work tirelessly to maintain it.

A sad fact of human nature is that if a group of people are put together without skilled leadership it is almost inevitable that conflict will emerge. Ambitions will clash, personal likes and dislikes emerge, blame will be apportioned and resisted – and so on.

It is one of the most important and most neglected functions of the leader to resolve conflict. Better still is to prevent it arising in the first place. Too many leaders turn their backs on disputes within their group and put it all down to inescapable human nature.

Conflict will be to a great extent prevented by the measures required to develop team working. They are:

- Setting clear objectives
- Setting standards
- Developing openness and frankness
- Rewarding co-operation and encouraging trust
- Making effective decisions
- Regular review.

■ Setting clear objectives

Objectives which all the team is aware of, understands and has helped to formulate make the difference between drifting along day by day, week by week simply responding to whatever the world throws at them. Working to objectives results in a proactive rather than reactive state of affairs, leading to improved effectiveness. It is only too easy to give way under the pressures of day-to-day work and to ignore the medium- to long-term future. Not only does this allow the world around us to change, leaving us behind, but it also inhibits team working.

A great stimulus to team working (and to general morale and enthusiasm) is to have something to aim at.

Working groups which do not have a target can be likened to a group of small boys kicking a football about on a piece of waste land. They dash about and use up lots of energy but never score any goals because there are no goal posts.

Setting objectives which mean something is not always easy and is only effective if approached in a methodical way with the application of some techniques. This is covered in the next chapter.

■ Setting standards

If individuals are left to decide the levels of quality and quantity of their work the result will be a patchwork. Some will be more easily satisfied than others. Also there will always be different ways to do a job and some people will cut corners.

The effective leader will agree standards and methods with his people to ensure that everyone works to a predictable norm which colleagues can depend on. Standards are important in reducing damaging conflict and loss of efficiency. This can be especially important in work which depends on a disciplined approach, as the following case illustrates.

Paying for Patrick's Paralysis

Patrick was taken on by a British company as Data Processing Manager. He took over a department of about twenty people and a mainframe computer. Patrick was a friendly character with a ready smile and a relaxed attitude to life in general. Everyone liked him. About six months after taking over the department Patrick had the task of revamping the computer systems and, in particular, designing and implementing some important new applications. This represented a major advance for computer use in the company and it meant that many antiquated and costly manual operations would be replaced. Patrick explained the objectives to his people and allocated work to his analysts and programmers. To meet the workload involved he also took on a skilled programmer/analyst for a contracted period of twelve months.

The work proceeded according to plan and was completed about fourteen months later. In the meantime one analyst had left and the contracted employee had moved on. Shortly after the systems were implemented the inevitable bugs began to appear and, also predictably, some of the 'user' departments asked for changes. That is when the troubles began.

Patrick had not agreed standards of documentation with his people. This meant that in some cases, including the work done by the two people no longer present, there was no record of how or why parts of the system were put together. The knowledge was in the heads of the people who had done the work, if they could remember it. The result was a marked inability to sort out the bugs or make the changes asked for. Programmers and analysts found themselves working in the dark trying to figure out how the various programs worked and the logic involved.

Those who had constructed adequate documentation resented the sloppiness of those who had not and rows developed as accusations and blame were thrown around. Personal relationships suffered and so did the work. It took about two years to clear up the mess and create the documentation for future reference. During this period more of the people left and Patrick found himself with a badly damaged reputation. The company lost time and money and getting the department back to team working required another year.

■ *Developing openness and frankness*

There are no secrets in an effective team. Everyone knows what is going on – good or bad. Developing an environment where people will be open and frank starts with the leader. No one goes through life without making mistakes and this includes the most high and mighty of leaders. If you, as leader, get something wrong you can encourage openness and frankness in your team by readily admitting your own mistake. If necessary apologise to your team. This will *not* reduce your standing or authority but trying to hide your failings will.

Try these tactics.

- Emphasise that if a failure is reported then something can be done about it. If it stays hidden it may fester and get worse.

- Ensure that everyone realises that reporting bad news will *not* result in hysterical reprimands, threats, warnings and the like.

  Demonstrate by example that bad news will be treated in a constructive way combined with sympathy and support for anyone who has blundered.

  The chances are that if someone gets something badly wrong it is *your* fault as leader. You may have delegated badly, provided poor or inadequate training, failed to agree standards, provided too few resources and so on. Gross negligence on the part of the employee is another matter but even then the leader's actions (or inaction) bear examination.

- Encourage your people to question your views and ideas (you do not have a monopoly of knowledge or genius) and be careful not to get ratty when they do. This will set the tone for the group as a whole and encourage team members to question each other without precipitating a blazing row. Make it clear that you consider questioning to be a helpful, supportive act and not a belligerent one.

Devil's advocate

Questioning can be used in a more formal way when something significant is in hand. Suppose someone has an idea, perhaps a plan for solving a tricky problem. A useful move is to allow the person to present the problem and proposed solution to one or more colleagues. The colleagues then act as devil's advocate by asking all the difficult questions they can think of. The idea is not to find fault with the ideas presented just for the sake of it but to help reveal any weaknesses *before* they are revealed by implementation. This is good for the individual and the team. If this is done in a supportive way with everyone keen to solve the problem effectively it will further encourage openness and frankness.

Put some humour into it!

Our jobs should be taken seriously but (except in the case of undertakers?) not solemnly. Seeing the funny side of a situation has the effect of reducing tension and often putting things into perspective. The effective leader will use humour to encourage people not to be afraid to say what they think. A solemn atmosphere can be inhibiting.

■ Rewarding co-operation and encouraging trust

One shrewd leader, finding that two of his people were not getting on too well, gave them a job to do together. The task was not easy and the outcome important. The objective was jointly discussed and agreed and the boss made it clear that he regarded both men equally responsible for the results. He was trying to form a team within a team and this, after a slightly shaky start, was what he got. The common aim forced both men to sort out their differences and work together. The reward was public recognition of their achievements and private recognition of the adult way in which they co-operated and supported each other.

■ Making effective decisions

An effective decision is one that produces the desired result with minimum fuss, cost and effort. This is more likely to be the result if more than one brain is applied. Teamwork is encouraged when the leader explains to his people that '*We* have a problem and *we* must decide how to solve it.'

Bring your people in and ask them for their ideas.

Don't leave anyone out who is in any way involved or likely to be affected. Don't overlook the fact that the most junior people are often at the sharp end and have a better idea of what actually goes on than more senior and more remote people. The observations and ideas of such people can be crucial and, remembering Likert's statement (page 47) about making things work, you need them backing you up. If they have a say in what to do they will be more committed to a successful result.

In addition, the effectiveness of a decision depends heavily on the amount of factual information available. Much of this information will be in the heads of your team members and you will need to get it.

■ Regular review

From time to time, *on a regular basis*, the team as a whole needs to review its activities. The review sessions should in particular cover these subjects:

- Objectives and the progress made to meet them
- Methods and systems and whether they are still appropriate

- Problems faced by individuals which need the help of other team members to be overcome.

If the team spends time considering such matters it will underline the concept of shared responsibility, give an opportunity for everyone to participate in determining the future action of the team and generally pull the group together.

The leader can also add a briefing element to the session to ensure that *all* team members are informed about matters that affect them and their jobs.

What should be included in the briefing?

Using the 'triple A formula' outlined below will put you on the right track and ensure that essential items are not overlooked:

- Achievements
- Administration
- Action

Under *achievements* the team can be informed of progress against budgets, output levels, sales achieved and the like. You can also mention individual achievements such as passing an examination, gaining a certificate of competency or completion of a difficult task. The briefing session is a good opportunity to give that highly motivating public recognition which the gurus recommend.

Administration includes such matters as changes to the pension scheme, holiday rotas or revised safety rules. Don't forget to allow ample opportunity for any questions on these and other matters. The briefing should not be a purely one-way traffic and, remembering Hertzberg's hygiene factors (see page 29), any grumbles must be heard, noted and acted upon.

Action refers to any activity which is not purely concerned with individual job content. It may cover extra, non-routine work such as preparations for visitors to the company or who does what in readiness for installing some new equipment. In other words, ensure that everyone knows what to do in respect to some one-off event.

The benefits of the review and briefing

The benefits both for the team and the leader fall into five categories.

Reduced misunderstanding

When people fully understand the objectives and purpose of the group and why things are happening around them the risk of muddles is greatly reduced. They can also act more intelligently in their everyday work especially when something unusual crops up requiring unusual action.

Increased co-operation with change

When people appreciate why change is necessary and know how they will be affected, they will more readily support it.

Improved commitment

When people fully understand and appreciate the importance of their contribution the likelihood of their giving their best increases. This is particularly so if they have had a chance to put forward their own views on what they should be doing.

Reduced damage resulting from rumours

Human nature means that speculation and rumour doing the rounds are almost always damaging. Dramatic stories are more exciting and entertaining and many people find a positive delight in passing them on.

Communicating the facts (even if less exciting) stops the damage in its tracks.

Strengthening the leader's role

The person who passes on official information comes to be regarded as the leader. This fact had costly results in parts of the British car industry in years gone by when announcements to employees were made via shop stewards. The workforce came to regard the shop stewards as their bosses and not the managers or directors of the company. The leader of a group strengthens his leadership by always giving briefings himself.

The VIP team leader – a special note

Chief executives and other very senior people have two team leader roles. The first is to develop team working among immediate subordinates: the directors and top managers. All the actions suggested in this chapter can be used for this purpose.

The second leadership role extends beyond the boardroom right down into the highways and byways of the organisation. Too often, particularly in large businesses, the top people are so remote from the workforce at large as to be virtually non-existent in their eyes.

Sir Algernon. Who's he?

Sir Algernon (not his real name) was chairman and chief executive of a medium-sized City of London company employing about a thousand people. The company had a number of offices all located within the 'square mile' and none more than a few minutes' walk from head office.

A consultant working with the company to find ways to improve profits was talking one day to a group of clerical workers in one of the smaller satellite offices. He referred to Sir Algernon and one of the clerks asked, 'Who is he?'

The consultant, surprised that an employee should not know the name of the chief executive, carried out a straw poll among the various offices.

He found that:

- Some 20 per cent of the employees did not know who Sir Algernon was

- Around 90 per cent of the employees had never seen him or said that they would not recognise him

- Only the more senior employees had any idea of what Sir Algernon did

- No one had any recollection of Sir Algernon ever visiting their offices

- Some people could remember being visited by the director responsible for their departments but this was so rare an occurrence that few remembered the name of the director concerned.

These facts were reported back to Sir Algernon who was both surprised and horrified. He pointed out that his picture appeared once in a while in the company newsletter but agreed that he was only visible in the flesh at the company Christmas party. He decided to go walkabout and confirmed the findings when very few people recognised him. One supervisor approached him saying, 'Can I help you? Are you looking for someone?'

Sir Algernon asked the consultant what he should do. The consultant recommended a regular 'Walking the Job' exercise by Sir Algernon *and* other senior people.

■ *What is 'Walking the Job'?*

Walking the job is an exercise in fact-finding, communication, motivation and team building. This is what to do:

1 Look ahead in your diary and allocate time to visit a part of the organisation (or all of it if it is not too large).

2 Turn up at the appointed time and make your presence known to the people in charge. It is usually best not to give warning of your intentions to make a visit as this will cause a lot of wasted time. Unless they are very confident (and trust in you) managers and supervisors will put their people on to 'tidying up', hiding problems and the like. This will give you a false impression of what life is really like in the engine room and irritate the employees.

However, you must not fail to inform the heads of sections or departments of your presence as failure to do so will undermine their position or, from their viewpoint, usurp their authority.

3 Now walk around the workplace talking and *listening* to the people. Watch out for the head of department who, wishing to ensure that no one says anything out of place, stands behind you mouthing answers that employees should give you in answer to your questions. Remember that some employees will be overawed and nervous, especially if they have not met you before. Start gently, perhaps by asking them what they do and asking them to show you. Most people enjoy talking about their jobs and, with the aid of some friendly questions, you can learn a lot.

Things to look out for are:

- The level of awareness of what the company does
- Awareness and understanding of policies
- Whether or not people are working to objectives and standards
- Problems that hinder their work
- Ambitions and hopes for the future
- Successes and failures
- Levels of morale
- Training or lack of it.

Do take the opportunity to praise and on no account make critical remarks or dish out reprimands.

What if something is wrong?

Anything that you spot which is not as you wish it to be should be reported to the person in charge and not the employees concerned. This should be done diplomatically without mentioning the names of employees who may have given you information which caused you concern. If that is unavoidable make it quite clear that the employee is not to be given a hard time because he or she told you. Any unwelcome comeback will ensure that you will never have the benefit of frankness in the future and no one will trust you again.

4 Have a look at the general conditions. Check:

- The state of the toilets
- The level of cleanliness of workplaces
- Adequacy of heating, lighting and ventilation
- Condition and suitability of furniture, equipment and machinery
- Refreshment facilities
- Notice-boards and what is on them
- Safety measures and standards.

If you find anything which is unsatisfactory do something about it – without delay. The cost could be small but the benefits large.

Remember

1 You are not on a fault-finding expedition. Anyone can wander round finding faults. Concentrate on opportunities for improvement, for encouragement, getting to know the people and letting them get to know you.

2 Have some questions worked out in advance. The questions should have a purpose and be linked to the objectives of the walkabout.

Random wandering accompanied by pointless comments and questions will waste your time and do nothing to enhance your reputation among the people you are seeing.

3 Don't turn your walkabout into a state visit.

State visits are much beloved of certain heads of large companies. They (both the visit and the VIPs) waste time and resources, damage their companies and benefit no one. The state visit has the following basic characteristics:

- It is primarily an ego trip for the big man or big woman.

- The visit is announced well in advance. This allows the managers of the branch being visited to see that all the staff are well briefed on what to say and what not to say. There is much cleaning, polishing and in one real-life case everyone was issued with new uniforms. These were taken away when the visit was over.

- The VIP arrives (often late) accompanied by an entourage of sycophantic assistants. These minions serve no apparent useful purpose (apparent, that is, to the workforce).

- The visit starts with refreshments and a meeting with the local boss and one or two of his or her lieutenants. Discussion during this meeting covers little of any consequence and is usually limited to expressions of admiration for the VIP.

- Eventually the VIP plus entourage make a quick trip round the branch. The VIP may ask a question or two of one or two token employees. Behind the VIP will be the local boss wearing a worried smile and ready to 'correct' any answers which are not 100 per cent what the VIP wants to hear.

- The VIP departs either to lunch or back to the comfort of head office, glad that the boring necessity of showing the flag is once again dealt with.

- The local boss may or may not receive a note from the VIP congratulating all and sundry on a job well done. The local boss may or may not pass this on to the workforce.

  In one real-life case the VIP spoke to no one but the local boss and made no comments of any kind. He did send a note later, pointing out that there was some litter in the car park!

This type of visit actually damages the team and does nothing to enhance the VIP's leadership role. It is better not to visit at all than go through the nonsense described. Visiting VIPs should:

1 Work out the objectives for the visit. What do you want to achieve? Possibilities are:

- To recognise good work

- To learn

- To show a real personal interest in what is going on

- To communicate good news

- To show support for local leaders

- To encourage.

2 Work out a programme for the visit which fits the objectives. Let the local boss know what you want to do and why. Tell the local manager that there should be no special preparations and that everyone should work normally.

3 Make sure that you are well briefed, for example,

- Names of key people at the branch

- Who does what
- Output, sales figures, or whatever is relevant
- Problems faced locally – both existing and past.

There is nothing more destructive to motivation than to approach someone who is proud of his or her work and to ask, 'Who are you and what do you do around here?'

4 Turn up on time and alone.

5 Talk to as many people as possible. Take a genuine interest in what they do and how they do it – it all contributes to the profits for which you are responsible.

Listen carefully to what is said and ask questions to draw them out. Use 'open' questions to encourage suggestions and to obtain opinion. Open questions are those that begin with words such as 'why', 'where' and 'how' and so avoid answers which are limited to 'yes' and 'no'.

6 Thank the people you have met and give praise where it is justified. Above all, be friendly, smile and be human.

7 Conclude by discussing your observations with local managers and supervisors. Again, the friendly approach will pay dividends. Thank the managers and give praise and encouragement.

8 When back in your VIP suite write a friendly letter to the branch manager summarising your reactions to the visit and asking for your thanks to be passed on to the workforce.

9 If you have made any promises take action to fulfil them without delay.

10 Brief your peers on your visit and plan the next one.

Was it a success?

Some analysis of what happened and to what extent you achieved your objectives will tell you if the visit succeeded. In addition ask yourself the question, 'Did I enjoy it?' If the answer is 'yes' you probably did a good job.

You will have another chance to measure your success rate when you go back again. If you are met by smiling people who are relaxed in your presence and talk to you frankly then you are showing the signs of effective leadership.

■ *A personal checklist for leaders at all levels*

It is easy, especially under pressure, to drift away from the practices which effective leadership demands. The drift can be subtle and we may not be aware of it. To prevent this becoming serious and to avoid the deadly risk of complacency it is useful to work through a checklist from time to time.

Ask yourself these questions.

Individuals	YES	NO
1 Am I consistently approachable – with the result that employees talk to me freely and openly?	☐	☐
2 Do I give support to my people when they have problems?	☐	☐
3 Do I take positive steps to help people overcome weaknesses and to use their strengths fully?	☐	☐
4 Do I see that everyone has challenging work?	☐	☐
5 Do I provide opportunities for people to learn?	☐	☐
6 Do I carefully explain what is required of people and why?	☐	☐
7 Do I give praise when earned?	☐	☐
8 Do I keep my promises to individuals?	☐	☐
9 Do I welcome, encourage and listen carefully to ideas from my staff?	☐	☐
10 Do I encourage people to challenge the status quo and what I do myself?	☐	☐

The team	YES	NO
1 Is there a well-understood set of objectives and standards for the team?	☐	☐
2 Have team objectives (and ways and means of achieving them) been constructed with the participation of the people?	☐	☐
3 Are team members consistently supportive of one another?	☐	☐
4 Do I regularly review progress with the team and brief them on what is going on?	☐	☐
5 Do I keep a watchful eye on the 'hygiene factors' (see page 29)?	☐	☐
6 Do I spot and deal effectively with any conflicts within the team?	☐	☐
7 Do I review workloads to ensure that there is a fair and sensible balance?	☐	☐
8 Do I organise my own work to have time available to develop further and maintain the team?	☐	☐

Summary of main points

1 Check how effective your people are as a team by using the questionnaire provided on pages 50-1.

2 The characteristics of a team (as opposed to a collection of people) can be identified and include such factors as:

- Group pride
- Willing mutual support
- A clear objective
- Subordinating individual ambitions to team success.

3 Teams must be created by leaders. Merely putting people together is not enough.

4 To create a team the leader must:

- Set objectives, with team participation
- Set standards, with team participation
- Develop trust, openness and frankness
- Encourage constructive criticism
- Reward co-operation
- Use all the talents present, for example, by involving the people in decision taking
- Regularly review objectives and progress with the team and brief them on the things that will affect them
- Watch the 'hygiene factors' (see page 29).

5 Walking the job is a valuable activity but only if done properly. VIPs who do this should avoid making state visits. They do more harm than good.

6 By using the checklist at the end of this chapter, leaders can test their effectiveness both in terms of the team as a whole and the individuals in it.

4 Objectives, Plans and the Effective Leader

Objectives (and the plans to meet them) not only provide challenge and other motivation to staff but also ensure that the business is actively controlled rather than passively drifting along. Ideally every business will have corporate objectives and a corporate plan. From these will be derived subsidiary objectives for divisions, departments, sections and individuals. Even if your company does not have business-wide objectives it need not inhibit you as a team leader from developing your own objectives and putting them into action. Providing that locally-devised objectives do not conflict with operations in other areas they can be effective and stimulate similar action elsewhere.

Corporate objectives

Top-level objectives are the responsibility of the top people. The objectives should be geared to long-term and strategic thinking and be derived from asking such questions as:

What business are we in?
This is not such a silly question as it sounds. You may, for example, manufacture fishing rods and regard this as the business you are in. However, you could also regard yourself as being in the leisure industry. This immediately opens the way to new thinking, such as

- Should we manufacture other sports products?

- What about buying and renting out fishing rights?
- Should we supply bait and other items for anglers?

The point is that having a narrow definition of the business inhibits useful diversification and can bring about dependency on a narrow product line. It is no accident that Marks & Spencer (the well-known retailer of clothing) also sells food and furnishings. It is no accident that Boots (the well-known chemist) sells records, videos, cameras and much more. Both of these successful companies recognised that they were in the *retail* business.

Being a seller of clothing is limiting. Being a retailer is not.

What position should we occupy in our industry?
Should we go for growth and aim to be the market leader? Would we be better off to stay as we are, even contract a little?

Should we diversify?
Are we vulnerable as we are? If we sell bacon can we also supply the eggs?

If we want to grow how do we do it?
Possibilities can include merger, acquisition or increased investment in our existing business.

The objectives which emerge from this kind of thinking will take account of a wide range of governing factors. Looking at these governing factors in detail may, in turn, require you to achieve some sub-objectives.

The governing factors might include:

- Company strengths and weaknesses (doing something about a weakness may be a prerequisite objective to achieving another)
- Threats and opportunities
- Economic and demographic forecasts
- Changes in public taste
- Technical developments

- Action of competitors
- Industry trends
- Political changes
- Company finances and the availability of capital

Departmental objectives

In order to achieve the corporate objectives each department will set its own objectives. These might include:

Finance   – Raising funds for expansion and/or achieving cash-flow improvements

Marketing   – Some market and marketing research

Production   – Improved output and quality levels

Distribution   – Reduced transport costs

Administration – Revised space utilisation

Personnel   – A training programme for certain employees and a recruitment drive.

Leadership skills employed at corporate level can therefore trigger off widespread activity and generate momentum throughout the business. This in turn adds excitement to the jobs of many people and it will have a motivating effect. It is vitally important though that everyone knows why the objectives have been set or the weary conclusion that it is change for no good reason will demotivate.

■ *What is a good objective?*

We could choose objectives in any old random fashion – if we are unwise enough to do so. We could also choose an objective which sounds good but in practice is largely a waste of time and resources. We could choose a good objective but fail to define it properly and spend time and money pursuing it with little to show for our efforts.

There are five criteria to be met when deciding on an objective:

The objective must be wholly relevant and carefully researched.
A British financial services company decided after much thought

that it needed to diversify. The company was heavily dependent on one major product and market and both were showing signs of weakening. An objective to diversify was agreed and a project team was set up to do the job.

Unfortunately the objective had not been researched sufficiently and the resulting diversification (although achieved) was in a market too restricted to produce any significant additional income. This was realised too late and should have been spotted before the project was implemented.

The same requirement of relevance and research also applies at departmental and sectional levels. The effective leader will choose objectives which make a real difference and check that this is so. Once the team realises that the objective is of little significance, enthusiasm for it will wane quickly.

The objective should be attainable but demanding.
One of the benefits of an objective is that it focuses attention on an issue. The energy and drive which can be generated should be concentrated on something fairly tough and not a small matter which should be sorted out as part of day-to-day work.

At the same time the objective, however difficult, must be attainable and seen to be so. Only blind faith will cause a team to follow its leader in pursuit of a hopeless cause – and blind faith is risky in business.

The objective must be clear and understandable.
All team members must understand what is to be achieved or they will have a limited chance of doing so. Consultation before deciding the objective and ample briefing after it is chosen are essential.

Vague 'statements of good intent' are not adequate as objectives and the sort of pronouncements often made by chairmen in company annual reports should be avoided. For example, 'The company will go forward employing its customer base within parameters governed by politico-economic constraints . . . blah . . . blah . . . .' This kind of nonsense is designed to please the less demanding shareholders and has nothing to do with real objectives.

A well-stated objective will contain no jargon.

The objective must take account of objectives or needs elsewhere in the organisation.
There is nothing to be gained by moving a bottleneck further down the line. This was discovered by a chemical manufacturing company in which one department computerised its activities. The objective of reducing delays in paperwork was achieved but another department which had to use the output could no longer cope. Although the total volume of transactions had not increased they now came through in big batches rather than in a steady flow. The problem was only solved when both departments were computerised.

The objective should be 'measurable', preferably at the level where action takes place.
A loosely-set objective to 'improve response time to customer enquiries' would be satisfied as soon as things are .0001 per cent better than before. Each objective should, as far as is humanly possible, be stated in precise mathematical terms and have a deadline.

The objective to improve customer service should read something like this: 'To respond to customer enquiries within four working hours. This standard to be achieved by 1 July.'

Such a statement makes clear *exactly* what is wanted and by when. The level of progress towards the objective can therefore be measured. Where possible, the results should be measured by the people doing the work. This is far better as a motivator than having the boss standing over the workers watching what is going on. The workers, especially if they have participated in choosing the objectives, are quite capable of self-monitoring. Doing it themselves removes a sense of oppressive supervision and enhances challenge as a motivator.

■ *What about the non-measurable objectives?*
There are some objectives, such as developing a team, which are difficult if not impossible to measure in mathematical terms. We

can, despite this difficulty, devise a means to monitor progress and know when our goal has been reached. The method is based on choosing a range of 'indicators' which characterise the situation when the objective has been reached.

Suppose, for example, our objective is to train and develop someone so that he or she has 'a positive attitude to the work', i.e., has pride in his or her work. We can probably think of another employee who already meets this objective and from this person's attitude we can derive the indicators we need.

They might include:

- Works to maximum personal ability most of the time
- Pays attention to detail and takes trouble to check that work is correct
- Finishes jobs on time, occasionally working late to get the job done
- Co-operates with colleagues
- Supports colleagues in difficulty.

When the employee we are focusing upon satisfies these requirements we can say that the objective has been reached.

■ *Where to look for worthwhile objectives*

From time to time objectives will present themselves as a result of your problems or aspirations. It is also a useful exercise to look for objectives on a regular basis as this will cause you to take stock of what is going on. Having such a rethink does not often happen in the face of day-to-day pressures without some special effort being made.

Just about every worthwhile objective will have a direct or indirect link to profits and the following are areas which are likely to offer fruitful opportunities:

- Production volumes
- Production costs
- Inventory levels
- Inventory turnover

- Accounts receivable/payable
- Bad debts
- Labour costs
- Return on investment
- Sales/market share
- Administration costs
- Sales costs.

Working out various ratios within these areas can also reveal the need for improvement and possibilities for increasing profits. Some of the following will have relevance to your business:

- Inventory as a percentage of annual sales
- Inventory as a percentage of total assets
- Sales: breakeven requirements
- Sales: estimated sales potential
- Total costs per unit produced
- Actual sales: forecast sales
- Scrap as a percentage of saleable product
- Downtime: productive time
- Sales value of production per man-hour
- Labour costs per unit produced
- Labour costs as a percentage of total costs
- Administration costs: total cost
- Administration costs: per unit produced
- Bad debts as a percentage of accounts receivable
- Average number of days to despatch of invoice
- Average days before payment is received
- Accidents per 100 man-days
- Labour turnover/retention.

The all-important plan

The most relevant and well-thought-out objective will gain little or nothing without a plan to achieve it. A common leadership fault is to neglect the planning side of things and to act as if deciding the objective will make it happen.

The plan itself is the means to the end required and is not an end in itself. It should:

- Lead to an improved situation for the business by aiding leaders to reach their objectives
- Assist individuals to work effectively
- Be flexible and allow changes to be made if required
- Include contingency arrangements to cater for a 'crisis'
- Encourage co-ordinated and mutually supportive action
- Enforce both groups and individuals to work systematically
- Reduce confusion and so reduce conflict and waste
- Provide milestones against which progress can be checked

What the plan should contain

The plan should start with a clear statement of the objective to be achieved. This simple and perhaps obvious provision is frequently neglected with the result that remarks such as these can be heard at a later date:

> *'I didn't think that the accounts department was included.'*

> *'No one told me this would be done before year-end.'*

> *'Why are we closing down the toolroom?'*

It is only too easy to lose sight of the objective especially if the time given to achieve it is lengthy. Writing it down helps to keep it in mind and prevents later arguments as to what it was!

The main body of the plan will include a schedule of the work to be done, by whom and when. This schedule forms the control element of the plan enabling everyone involved to be able to see what they must do and what colleagues must do.

A series of checklists of action is a useful or even essential item to support the overall programme. The programme itself is best produced in diagram form along the lines of the figure on page 78. The diagram includes a time-scale and the various actions to be taken at different stages. It is a simplified version of what the plan might be for the implementation of a computer system. The objective is to go live in week 12/13.

In addition to listing the work to be done the diagram shows:

- The sequence of the tasks
- The time allowed for each one
- The interdependence of the tasks.

For example, training cannot start until all the preparations for it are complete *and* the hardware is available.

One of the main advantages of using a diagram is that any slippage and how this will affect the plan as a whole can be spotted. If, for instance, you see around week 6 that training preparations are not proceeding fast enough you will know that it may in turn delay the training itself and, even if the hardware installation and testing are up to scratch, the programme will not be completed in time. Spotting this allows the team leader to switch resources or take some other remedial action. The diagram can also be seen by all the team members and those responsible for training will know they are out of step. They will thus be aware that they need to do something about it without having to be told by the boss.

Who is responsible?

There should be no doubt about who is expected to carry out each of the tasks included in the plan. Names or initials can be included in the diagram or separate lists can be issued showing who is doing what. Never allow any doubt to creep in or something will either slip through the net ('I thought Jane was doing the ordering'), or will be duplicated ('How the hell did we get two of these?').

What have we got to do the job?

Another part of the leader's job is to ensure that the plan takes

PROJECT PLAN IN DIAGRAMMATIC FORM

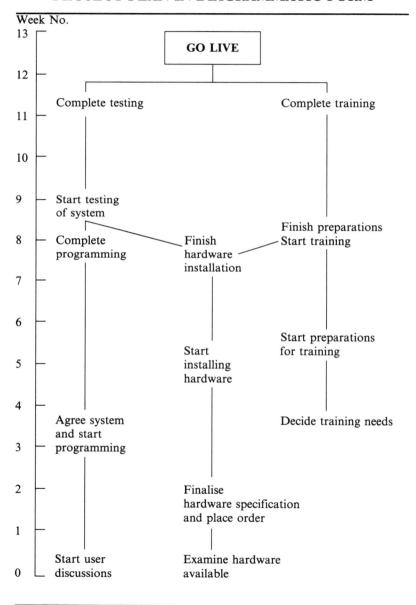

Week No.

13 — GO LIVE

12 —

11 — Complete testing   Complete training

10 —

9 — Start testing
     of system
                                      Finish preparations
8 — Complete   Finish   Start training
     programming   hardware
                    installation

7 —

6 —
                                      Start preparations
                    Start   for training
5 — installing
     hardware

4 —
     Agree system   Decide training needs
     and start
3 — programming

2 — Finalise
     hardware specification
     and place order
1 —

     Start user   Examine hardware
0 — discussions   available

account of the resources available and that everyone knows what they are. A budget is almost always an important requirement as this not only enforces careful consideration of what is really essential in the way of equipment and labour but also ensures that people know what the constraints are.

The people available, the computer time which can be taken for testing, the production machinery, vehicles and space are all examples of resources to be identified and included.

Suppose something goes wrong?

It is rare for any plan of any magnitude not to hit a snag somewhere along the line. People go sick, prices rise, machines break down and politicians can move the tax and legal goalposts.

This means that:

- Flexibility should be built into the plan or at least rigidity excluded from it
- Contingency plans need to be drawn up in advance.

A useful exercise is for the team to have a session on 'what-ifs'. Before the plan is finally approved some useful questions can be asked, for example:

- What if the trainer goes sick?
- What if the programming is not completed on time?
- What if there is a transport strike?
- What if there is a supplier strike?
- What if VAT is increased?
- What if we cannot get adequate insurance?

In real life some of the problems which might arise are extremely difficult or impossible to evade by means of contingency plans. If Iraq invades Kuwait there is not much that you can do about it. It is equally unlikely that you can forecast it! Despite this limitation there is always a number of steps which can be taken either to evade the problem or to limit the damage which might be caused. Plans should therefore include where possible such fall-back measures as:

- All key players having an understudy
- Alternative transport plans (if your lorry breaks down know in advance where to hire one)
- Alternative suppliers
- A manual alternative to a computer system
- Stand-by storage facilities
- A press release or letter to customers, drafted in advance
- A bank overdraft facility.

It is also good policy to build into your time-scale a 'contingency allowance' of say 10 per cent so that you have a safety margin for small delays. However, this must not be used as an easy option and it should be made clear to all that rewards will go to those who keep a little ahead of the game rather than a little behind.

At all events you should be ready to switch horses quickly if the need arises. This is where a good monitoring system comes in.

Keeping track of events

Every step in the implementation of your plan should be monitored to see that what you intended to happen is actually happening. Once some aspect of the work has gone seriously adrift achieving the objective could be jeopardised. This is especially so when the job is a complex one involving lots of interdependent actions. What then are the essential features of an effective monitoring system?

1 'Measurement' is delegated to the lowest possible level.
This means that you, the leader, make sure that your people know what is required and that *they* monitor it. You will not need to know if every little item is going along nicely, only if it is not. Leave the monitoring to the people who are at the sharp end along with delegated power to take corrective action which lies within their own area of influence.

This form of delegation is a form of good leadership. It shows people that you trust them and giving them the freedom to decide what action to take is motivating. If you are doing all the monitoring and calling all the shots it will be regarded as interference and there is all the difference between that and supervision.

2 The monitoring must be wide enough and well balanced.
Take care to avoid concentrating on only some parts of the plan. There is a natural tendency to keep an eye on the exciting bits such as sales made or output levels. The more prosaic activities should be routinely monitored and the progress of each checked against the overall plan.

3 Feedback must be timely
Any event (or non-event) which is not entirely in accordance with the plan should be spotted without delay. The earlier a problem is reported the better are the chances of taking remedial action. The monitoring system should be designed to pick up trends as soon as they are evident.

4 Reporting must be accurate and precise.
Data collected for monitoring purposes must be accurate and reported in minimum form. Mountains of computer printout providing every detail can only be used with a lot of effort and it all takes time. Summaries or exception reports (what is out of line) will be easier to use.

The data that you choose to monitor events should generally be:

- As few as possible
- Capable of resulting in action
- Helpful in forecasting what is likely to happen
- Capable of being compared with some standard or benchmark.

A Brussels-based manufacturing company had branches throughout Europe. An objective to increase the sales of certain products was decided upon and a great deal of preparation went into a new sales and marketing plan. Stocks were delivered to strategically placed warehouses, salesmen briefed, new literature distributed and advertising was stepped up.

The weakness in the scheme was the monitoring system. A number of top executives insisted on progress reports in very great detail. A complicated computer system was designed which required a lot of input from the branches. The result was:

- Backlogs of recording at the branches

- Delays in reporting results

- Computer reports which were incomplete.

These reports were extremely lengthy and very difficult to use and, because of their incompleteness, misleading. To make matters worse there was no way of knowing at the centre that data was held up at a branch and not included. The result was a great deal of confusion, frustration and anger, especially when the VIPs accused the branches of not doing well enough. Branch staff knew just by looking at the stock in their warehouses that they were selling very effectively. Possibly a reporting system based on stock levels would have been a quicker and more accurate method – and cheaper too.

A special word on accuracy

Some data need to be reported with a high degree of accuracy but some do not. The question to ask yourself is 'How accurate must we be to make an effective decision?'

In a real-life case a group of people were dealing with transactions, each of which required a file. An objective was agreed that each transaction should be dealt with within an agreed period of time and that any backlogs should be reported so that remedial action could be taken. Each employee was instructed to list the files they had (each day), and put against each one the date when the file was opened. The list was then sent to a central point where the information was entered on to a computer. The computer then produced a report showing the status of each person's workload. A copy of this report was then sent back to the employee!

As one employee said, 'I spend valuable time filling in the form and the computer then tells me what I already know.'

The fact was that it mattered little if someone was ten files adrift or fifteen files adrift. The same action was called for in either case. It was only necessary for the employees to look at the pile of overdue files to know if the situation was getting out of hand.

The same principle applies with other types of data. For example, if the cost of doing something works out at £951.37 it is unlikely that this would be treated any differently from information that the cost was 'approximately £950'.

In other words accuracy should be sufficient to trigger off appropriate action. Time-consuming and expensive analysis to provide a figure to three decimal places is often wholly unnecessary.

■ Choosing your monitoring methods

In addition to the need for accuracy, timeliness and so on there are other criteria which should govern your choice of method for keeping track of events:

1 The least costly

2 The least laborious

3 Visible to as many people as possible

4 Simplicity.

Avoid the temptation to set up a complicated recording and reporting system. With a little imagination it is almost always possible to find a cheap and easy way to do it – and one which is effective.

The bureaucratic disease

The management of a hospital wanted more information on the ailments which were being treated in an outpatients department. In order to obtain the information the medical staff were provided with a supply of forms to be filled in, one for each patient.

In accordance with the usual knee-jerk reaction of form designers each form asked for 'standard' information such as:

- Name and address of patient
- Sex

- Date of birth
- National Insurance number
- Next of kin, and so on

The forms, after completion, were batched and sent to a clerical department for summarising and for sending a report to go to the manager.

Strenuous complaints were received from the very busy medical staff who felt they had better things to do than fill in forms. The system was reconsidered and the realisation dawned that the *only* information needed was the ailment being treated. All the patient's personal details were redundant information for the purposes of the exercise (and were in any case recorded elsewhere).

The result was the provision of a box divided into compartments, each of which was labelled with a common ailment. Once diagnosis was completed all the doctor or nurse had to do was drop a plastic disc into the appropriate compartment. At the end of each day someone counted the discs and the required information was available.

Some tried and trusted methods

The wall chart
Perhaps the most obvious wallchart is a large copy of the plan diagram placed where all concerned can see it.

A constant visual reminder of what is to be done and by when helps to keep things on track and the effect is greater if coloured markers are used to show when tasks or stages have been completed. Any unfinished job which is nearing (or has passed) its 'do-by' date will be apparent.

Graphs and bar charts
These can be used to show cumulative figures such as sales, production, money received or any kind of completed transaction. If a target is marked on the graph this will show people how they are getting on and what still needs to be done.

Any kind of visual display enables the team leader to check progress at a glance without any reporting back by employees or asking questions of them. The latter can be irritating, threatening and demotivating.

The physical evidence
Frequently, progress is marked by physical changes such as stock building up in a warehouse. There is no need to record this on paper if the stock is stored in lots of pre-determined amounts so that its size can be assessed by quick visual inspection. A row of say, fourteen piles each containing ten pallet loads can be rapidly evaluated and compared with a target figure.

The team leader, when walking the job, can see for himself or herself how things are going.

Other physical evidence which can do the job for you might be:

- The number of delivery notes
- The size of a pile of unpaid invoices
- The number of bins filled with scrap or rejects
- The number of empty (or full) tables in your restaurant.

Progress meetings
The review/briefing meeting can be a useful monitoring method providing it is well conducted. One effective leader holds a ten-minute feedback session every morning, with all present standing up. This reduces the readiness of the participants to indulge in unnecessary chit-chat and consequent time-wasting.

In a different context another effective leader holds a regular Friday afternoon feedback session. This longer session works to a precise agenda in which each person reports his or her own progress. The advantages in this case include:

- The opportunity for co-ordination of activities
- The ability for *all* to see when mutual support is required.

Progress meetings also enable the leader to ask supplementary questions and for participants to explain or describe events which are out of the ordinary.

To save time it is good policy to make reporting at meetings on an exception basis. If everything is going according to plan it is only necessary to say so without going into all the details. Only exceptions to the plan need be described and discussed.

■ *What if the plan or the objective was wrong?*
Sometimes we can be some way down the line when we realise that the objective may not be the right one. This can be as the result of an error of judgement at the outset or because circumstances have changed in the meantime. There are any number of external influences which may have changed the situation, for example, competitors' actions, tax changes or even the weather! Alternatively we may find that the plan is flawed in some way, no longer suits changed circumstances or that experience has revealed a different opportunity.

Whatever the case, the effective leader will recognise and accept the situation and will change the objective, the plan or both. One of the most demotivating actions is for a leader to insist on stubbornly pressing on when everyone in the team realises that it is a lost cause. The credibility of the leader will be the first casualty as certain politicians have found to their cost.

Summary of main points

1 Objectives and the plans to meet them provide direction and control – and offer a means to motivate members of the team.

2 Ideally there will be a corporate objective governing the direction of the entire organisation and from which divisional and departmental objectives will be derived.

3 Even if no higher-level objectives exist the effective leader will, with team participation, set objectives for his or her own area of responsibility.

4 A good objective (i.e., one which is really effective and not just a gesture to good leadership) will meet five criteria: relevance, attainability, clarity, measurability and in tune with the rest of the organisation's objectives.

5 Some objectives may be 'non-measurable' – at least in a quantitative sense. There are ways to overcome this apparent obstacle.

6 A well-thought-out and detailed plan is needed if there is to be any real chance of achieving an objective. The plan will also need to meet a number of criteria and is best illustrated by means of time-scale diagrams.

7 The plan must clearly show who is responsible for what and by when. This information must be widely communicated.

8 The plan must also take account of financial and other resources available and include contingency actions. Some 'what if? thinking is necessary.

9 A tailor-made monitoring system is needed to keep track of progress and to provide adequate warning of any adverse trends in sufficient time for remedial action to be taken.

10 Monitoring is most effective if delegated as far down the hierarchy as possible and ideally will be carried out at the sharp end by the people doing the work.

11 Monitoring must be planned to meet some basic criteria – especially to ensure that feedback is such that any necessary action *can* be taken *and* will achieve the required result.

12 The accuracy of feedback data needs careful consideration. Too great a demand for accuracy can result in unnecessary cost, extra work, irritation and no improvement in the control of activities.

13 A number of tried and tested monitoring methods are suggested (pages 84–6).

14 Neither objectives nor plans should be carved in tablets of stone. Both may need to be changed and effective leadership avoids rigidity and obstinate adherence to a failing system.

5 Communicating – It's Not Just Telling Them

Various forms of communication such as walking the job and briefing sessions have already been mentioned. However, there is much more to it than has been covered and the effective leader needs to employ every proven method or technique available.

Perhaps you rate yourself as a good communicator – most of us do! Try the following self-check questionnaire to see if there are any areas for improvement.

	YES	NO
1 Do you praise your staff as readily as you criticise them?	☐	☐
2 Do you communicate equally often with all your people, juniors as well as seniors?	☐	☐
3 Do you hold regular, planned meetings in addition to *ad hoc* emergency sessions?	☐	☐
4 Do your staff *consistently* tell you what you need to hear and not just what they think you would like to hear?	☐	☐
5 Do your people communicate effectively with each other?	☐	☐

		YES	NO
6	Have you reviewed and reconsidered your communication needs and methods within the last twelve months?	☐	☐
7	Do you and all your people, have an up-to-date job description?	☐	☐
8	Have you had formal training in leading group discussion?	☐	☐
9	Do you run a formal grievance procedure?	☐	☐
10	Do you believe that you are aware of the problems of your staff?	☐	☐
11	Do all your people know how their work contributes to the work of the business as a whole?	☐	☐

A 'no' or a 'not sure' answer to any of these questions indicates an area which can do with some thought. Cross-check your results by ticking the boxes for these questions:

		TRUE	FALSE
1	Our notice boards are tidy and up-to-date.	☐	☐
2	I never hear comments such as:	☐	☐
	'Nobody told me.'		
	'I didn't know it was my job.'		
	'What are these forms for?'		
3	In the last six months we have not had any foul-ups caused by 'misunderstandings'.	☐	☐
4	I am always aware of how my department is performing against targets and standards.	☐	☐

If, having considered your answers to the questions, you feel that communication can be improved it is worth going back to the basics. Whatever you want to communicate and whatever the circumstances there are two areas which require attention before you have any hope of real success. These are preparation and transmission.

▌ Preparation

Just two minutes' thought about what you are going to say, how and why you are going to say it, can make all the difference between communicating and not communicating. If you can find more than two minutes so much the better. Think about:

The purpose
Ask yourself why you are about to communicate. What do you want to achieve? In particular ask the question 'What message' (idea) do I want them to go away with?' Considering this question will help to focus what you are going to say – avoiding weakening the message with side issues or padding.

If you are not absolutely clear what your message is before you start it is likely that your 'audience' will not be clear when you have finished.

The other person's viewpoint
Consider carefully what the other person is likely to be feeling. How would you react in his or her shoes?

Our reactions to information received are influenced by our own wants and personal objectives. We are also affected by our personal experiences and we particularly remember bad things which have happened to us. This means that we *must* think about how the people on the receiving end will interpret our words and what meanings they will put on them.

In one case a manager announced that all the secretaries and typists in his organisation would be equipped with word processors. Each typewriter, as it came to the end of its life, would be replaced by a word processor and the appropriate person trained in word processing. The manager took great care to emphasise the benefits to the employees, including an increase in salary for each one who completed the training successfully.

The announcement was received with little enthusiasm and within twenty-four hours the plan was being vigorously opposed. The manager was puzzled as he genuinely believed that the idea was a good one for the employees as well as the company. Enquiries revealed that two of the employees had formerly been made redundant as a result of mechanisation (including word processing) in previous jobs. These employees had quickly made their fears known to their colleagues who commented that nothing had been said about job security. They interpreted this silence as evidence that jobs would be at risk. After all, the manager had made much of the improved productivity which word processing would bring!

The project had to be explained again with public reassurances about job security. However, the damage was done and a great deal of patience was needed to implement the scheme and it took a long time before suspicion died away. It could be argued that an effective leader would have known enough about his or her people to be aware that two of them had experienced redundancy in similar circumstances. In any case, he or she might have anticipated some worries and done something to prevent the fears arising.

Where and when

Minor or routine announcements can probably be satisfactorily made at regular briefing sessions. Consideration should be given to the timing. It is not a good idea simply to say, 'I'll tell them at the meeting on Friday.' This is particularly the case when an announcement from above needs to be passed on. If there is any chance at all that some other leader will tell his or her people before you tell yours then you have the recipe for trouble.

Your people will hear it from someone else's people. This means that they may hear a distorted version of the message *and* they will feel let down. 'Why is it we always find out from gossip in the canteen or corridors first?' is a common complaint. What it implies to the staff is that you, the leader, don't think they are important enough to be told when their colleagues elsewhere are told.

More significant matters may well need a special arrangement. But do be careful about the when and where of these too.

The chief executive of one company decided to give his senior personnel a briefing on a new corporate plan. He decided, probably rightly, that this should be face to face. About fifty managers were told to assemble at a conference centre about half a mile from the offices at 6.30 p.m.

The official end of the working day was 5.30 p.m. although most of the managers worked on to 6.00 or even later. Notwithstanding this there was general indication that *whether they liked it or not* they would be kept late on the night in question. Having assembled at 6.30 they were kept waiting until about 7.00 p.m. before anything happened. The explanation of the corporate plan, preceded by a rambling summary of past events, was finally completed at about 8.30 when an opportunity was given for questions to be asked.

By this time the audience was tired, hungry and wanted to go home. Very few had any inclination to prolong the agony by asking questions. Those who did were the usual sycophants who used questions to draw attention to themselves, and the odd difficult personality who could not resist splitting a few hairs.

The chief executive did not get the enthusiastic response he was looking for. He might have considered the feelings of the audience and also taken the view that since the corporate plan was of major importance it should have been explained in prime time. As someone remarked, 'The corporate plan affects our lives in the office and we should have been told in the office.'

■ *Brief and to the point*

In the above case the essential points in the corporate plan could have been covered in about thirty minutes. The preceding summary could have been left out as could much of the detail which the people could have read for themselves later.

A good rule for ensuring that you get the message over is to work out what you want to say, write it down and then cut it by at least 30 per cent. Remove all unnecessary words, padding and any lengthy facts and figures. The latter will probably not be remembered in any case.

■ *The structure*

Having decided what you intend to say decide how you are going to say it. The sequence will be important especially if the message is a long one.

A good old rule is, 'Tell them what you are going to say, say it and then tell them what you said.' This does not mean a load of agonising repetition. It does mean starting with a brief statement of the message (preferably with an attention-grabbing point), following with the detail and then finishing with another brief, attention-grabbing summary.

For instance:

'We have had the best year ever (pause) but we face a problem. I am going to explain the problem and tell you how we will overcome it.'

The listeners now know what the subject is to be and, hopefully, are stimulated by enough curiosity to listen.

At the end of the explanation a summary such as this could be used:

'You are now all aware of the problem presented to us by this new competitive product. You also know what we are going to do about it – to make sure that next year is even better than the last.'

The last sentence of the concluding statement ends the communication on a high note and restates the sort of objective which might have been set out by the leader.

The message will have more force if it builds, point by point, in a logical way with attention-grabbing statements introducing each point. This structure also enables the leader to end with an underlying message which the listeners will take away with them.

Transmission – or putting it over effectively

Careful preparation and consideration of the likely views of the audience will go a long way to ensuring that what you say is what they hear. There are, though, a number of simple but necessary techniques to adopt.

Visual aids

It is true that a picture is worth a thousand words and a well-drawn graph, pie chart or bar chart is much more effective than a barrage of figures.

It has been said that only about 30 per cent of spoken information is absorbed and remembered by listeners. A visual equivalent is reckoned to increase understanding and retention to about 70 per cent. This applies not only to relatively complex matters such as financial analyses or the results of an extensive statistical exercise. Less dramatic requirements such as how to fill in a form are more effectively explained with, say, a large-scale mock-up on a flip-chart sheet.

Overhead projectors, slides and videos are also effective in the right places and don't forget demonstrations as a way to capture attention and get the message across.

Watch the tempo

Don't go too fast. This raises the risk of losing your audience. You may find the subject quite straightforward but the listener may not and once someone fails to take in a point then he or she will probably switch off. Conversely, going too slow can make you dull and boring.

Be enthusiastic

If the leader wants enthusiasm from the team then the leader must also be enthusiastic. Put plenty of pep into what you are communicating. This will also make your point more interesting and much more likely to be assimilated.

Avoid unfamiliar jargon

Every industry, company or job has its own particular jargon. Bear in mind that any jargon you may use may not be familiar to all the listeners or even to any of them.

If technical terms are unavoidable be sure to explain them if there is any doubt that someone may not know what they mean.

● *Is it all talking?*

The emphasis so far has been on spoken words. There are of course ways to communicate using the written word. These include:

- Notice-boards
- Memoranda
- Leaflets
- Letters included in pay packets
- Company newsletter or in-house magazines.

The advantages of such methods are that they are cheap and it is possible to ensure that the statements made are accurate. It is also possible, since you usually have enough time, to choose some careful wording which is concise, clear, unambiguous and comprehensible to the recipients. The language should be 'reader-friendly' and informal. Avoid phrases such as these, which turn the reader off:

'It has come to my notice that . . .'

'Due to unforeseen circumstances . . .'

'Contrary to the evidence of data . . .'

'Staff will take notice that . . .'

'Employees are reminded that . . .'

'Consequent upon unfavourable trading conditions . . .'.

The disadvantages of notice-boards, memoranda and the like are that they are:

- Impersonal
- Do not allow for questions to be asked
- Depend upon the reader's interpretation which, if wrong, cannot be immediately put right.

Notice-boards, unless carefully controlled, may have unofficial notices stuck on them – including in one company a spoof notice advising of reduced holiday entitlement! Pencilled additions by the company humorists and barrack-room lawyers can also be a problem even if their graffiti are normally more entertaining than the notice they are scrawled on.

Despite these problems the notice-board, if properly supervised and up-to-date, has a place.

■ Addressing the five thousand

We can have some sympathy with the chief executive of a major organisation who knows that it would be good if he or she could talk face to face with all the company's people but cannot find a way to do it. Mass meetings in the car park are an expensive way to bring production to a halt and addressing five hundred groups of ten people one after another would take all year.

Sadly, most VIPs resort to the cascade system with all its attendant dangers. Here is an example of what can go wrong and how good intentions can be misunderstood.

Chairman to Managing Director
Profits are falling and I wish to address all the employees in the works canteen on Wednesday at 9.00 a.m. I want to describe the difficulties that the company faces and the action we will be taking to put matters right.

If the canteen is too small to accommodate all the employees any overflow can be provided with chairs in the corridor outside. A public address system should be set up so that they can hear.

Managing Director to Works Director
By order of the Chairman all employees will assemble in the canteen at 9.00 a.m. on Wednesday to be told about falling profits. Employees who cannot get in will sit in the corridor and listen to the talk on the loudspeaker.

Works Director to General Manager
The Chairman is to speak to the employees about falling profits in the corridor outside the canteen on Wednesday at 9.00 a.m.

General Manager to Foreman
Canteen profits are falling and the Chairman will tell everyone about it in the corridor at 9.00 a.m. on Wednesday.

Foreman to Shop Stewards
The canteen is making no profit and will be closed from
Wednesday. Everyone can eat in the corridor.

Shop Stewards to Employees
The canteen is closed and they seem to expect us to eat sandwiches
in the corridor. This is a diabolical erosion of conditions and a
ballot for strike action will be taken . . .

This apocryphal tale is an example of the extended lines problem.
But is there a practical alternative which brings the VIP closer to
the workforce? One possible approach is described in *The Renewal
Factor* by Robert H. Waterman (Bantam Press).

Waterman reports on how Cummins Engine (USA) goes about
communicating and quotes Henry Schacht, the Chairman, as
follows:

> *'Knowledge is liberating,' Schacht says. 'We spend a lot
> of time communicating the absolute facts of our business
> to all our folk, right down to the most recently hired
> person in the office or on the shop floor. Jim Henderson
> [Managing Director] makes hour-long tapes four times a
> year that are followed by question and answer sessions
> with groups of employees, fifty at a time, until the whole
> workforce is briefed. We found out that hierarchical
> information passing is impossible,' Schacht said. 'By the
> time the message gets passed down from the person who
> attended the staff meeting to the people who need to
> know, it is so diluted and different it is worthless.'*

Here we have an example of the use of a little imagination. A
taped message may be equated to a written message but there is a
big difference. An hour-long message on tape would take up a lot
of words and space on paper and although many people would
regard an hour as rather too long the listening will be easier than
the equivalent reading. The Managing Director's voice, even on
tape, is also more personal.

The question and answer sessions used by Henderson satisfy one of the criteria for successful communication: it should be a two-way process. This is not always easy to achieve, especially if some people are not used to group discussion. Let's look at this in the context of departmental meetings or briefings.

■ The two-way process in a group

If the Martians are invading the required communication is likely to be quick, one-way and authoritative. If we want to mould our people into a team a slower, two-way (or multi-way) and democratic process is needed.

Suppose you have your team carefully seated around you. Unless you have been through the discussion process a number of times before some people may well be reluctant to participate. The reasons can include:

Absence of a common interest or objective
You may think that rescheduling the shift system is a great idea. The team members may not.

You may be concerned about the company image, customer service or whatever but the employees may have entirely different concerns. Salary levels, job security, pensions, holiday entitlements and the like may be the subjects they would really like to talk about.

Fear of a lack of direction
Even very senior managers who have spent most of their working lives in an environment in which they have been directed may fear participation in decision making. The implied responsibility may be unwelcome and some people may doubt their ability to cope in a situation where they are expected to contribute ideas.

Suspicion
There may be people who are suspicious of your motives. If, in particular, group discussion is not something they are used to they may suspect that:

- You are trying to pull a fast one
- You are not really interested in their views and the meeting is just window-dressing

- There is something sinister going on.

This last point was exemplified by the company which arranged a number of group discussions on potential future changes. These changes involved considerable rearrangement of people and jobs with a vague possibility of redundancies in the background. Certain people, encouraged to speak frankly, expressed opposition to some or all of the ideas under discussion.

These people were later told that they had made it clear that they were not committed to the company and its future and would be made 'redundant'. Perhaps needless to say, this action effectively destroyed any willingness on the part of the staff to communicate their opinions when asked.

Perception of the leader
Differences in age, accent, sex, dress, social background and many other factors can influence our perception of another person. Everyone has prejudices and stereotypes and these influence reactions to what is being communicated.

Messages can become distorted – often because a preconceived opinion about the person giving it determines the interpretation.

What must we do?
First, recognise that barriers will exist and that a lot of patience may be required of you, the leader.

Positive steps may be required to overcome the barriers, for example:

1 A lack of interest in an objective might be overcome by explaining how the self-interest of the individuals is compatible with the success of the group of which they are a part. Whilst high company profits are not a guarantee of generous pay awards they at least offer the opportunity. The converse is also true – a loss-making company is in no position to be generous.

2 Fears of being unable to cope or accept responsibility in a participative situation may be overcome by reassurances that no one expects miracles and even the smallest contribution will be gratefully received.

3 The teeth of suspicion can be drawn by the leader. If you think it likely that some of your people are suspicious of your motives then express the suspicions yourself. Get the whole thing into the open and show that you have nothing to hide. In many cases the fears that people have are irrational and talking about them often makes this clear.

Above all, and it is worth repeating, be patient. Resistance to something may not be rational but it is understandable and trust in you, the leader, will not appear in a day. Your effectiveness as a leader will grow as trust in you grows and you may have to change in order to earn it.

Practical steps in leading a group session

The objective in preparing for and conducting the session is to achieve a constructive result. This will be most likely if the environment is relaxed and friendly and everyone knows what the purpose of the meeting is. The following actions will help.

1 Arrange the meeting on familiar or, at least, neutral ground. The manager's office or an imposing boardroom may not be conducive to a relaxed atmosphere.

2 Prepare an agenda and provide all participants with a copy well in advance.

3 Choose the participants with care. A really lively multi-way discussion is not likely to be effective if more than a dozen or so people are present *but* do not leave out any key people. Status or rank are not necessarily the right criteria for deciding who should participate and the office junior may be a priority choice.

4 Choose a time which is least inconvenient to the participants and make sure everyone knows the starting time *and the finishing time*. The time required will to some extent be governed by the subject to be dealt with but a limit of about 1½ hours is recommended. It is difficult to maintain commitment and interest beyond

this and having a lot of available time will only encourage people to ramble on.

5 Arrange the seating in an informal way. A circle is more conducive to multi-way discussion than the boardroom-table style. You, the leader, should be visible to all but your position should suggest you are first among equals rather than a big tycoon.

6 Make sure that you have all the necessary visual aids, documents, handouts or whatever ready.

A flip-chart or blackboard may be needed to illustrate the subject to be discussed and also as a means for participants to describe something.

■ Running the session

As leader, your primary role is to encourage creative action. This requires skilled chairmanship involving gentle but firm control of the meeting and keeping everyone to the subject. Your role should be careful listening, co-ordinating the people and stimulating thinking by means of skilful questioning. Be especially careful not to monopolise the meeting with your own views. This will either kill discussion stone dead or result in arguments.

The following actions will help you:

Start with a reiteration of the programme of the meeting and what you hope will be achieved
This may involve describing a problem to be solved or an opportunity to be exploited. This can often be best done by some facts and figures on a flip-chart sheet. The flip-chart can then be left visible to the group throughout the session to act as a point of reference. This helps to avoid time-wasting digression.

Avoid at the outset being too positive or too detailed about what you want
Suggest guidelines rather than a very precise definition. Put forward your objective as a cock-shy and make it clear that you are open to ideas for alternative objectives and alternative ways and means to go about achieving them.

A statement such as this may be along the right lines: 'We need to look at ways to improve our level of customer service – perhaps by starting off with identifying what we mean by customer service.' Such an opening provides an opportunity to break the subject down into manageable headings such as response to enquiries, delivery standards, customer assistance and spare parts availability.

Have some questions ready to stimulate participation
The questions should be of the 'open' variety (i.e., they cannot be answered by a 'yes' or 'no'). For example:

> *'Which aspect of customer service needs most attention?'*
>
> *'Which aspect can be improved at least cost?'*
>
> *'How can we improve delivery times?'*
>
> *'In what ways could training help?'*

Treat people as individuals
There may be obstacles to participation which are personal to some of the individuals present. They may:

- Be a little overawed by the occasion
- Be shy or lack fluency
- Feel unable to put opinions forward in the presence of more senior people
- Be afraid of having their ideas criticised or laughed at
- Not be used to the participative style of management

Make it clear that you value everyone's comments equally and, if someone is clearly reluctant to speak, direct a friendly question to that person. For example: 'George, you are in the warehouse most of the time and you must see a lot of what goes on. What do *you* think is the cause of the problem?' Such questions, put directly to an individual, can pay dividends. On one occasion a group had been discussing a problem for a considerable time without making any real progress. One participant, the most junior person present, had said nothing. The leader noticed this and put a question directly to him. The reply, although diffident, provided the solution to the problem, which the participant was aware of all the time.

Later, when the session was over the leader asked the man concerned why he had not spoken earlier. He replied, 'No one asked for my opinion and I did not think it was my place to say anything in front of all those important people.'

Summarise and clarify as you go along
Many thousands of words can be spoken at a meeting and not everyone will be clear about, or remember, what has been agreed. As soon as there is a consensus on something summarise it and write it up on the flip-chart. This will confirm the matter and can act as another reference point for further discussion on other aspects.

A series of agreements written up will also encourage the group who will see that they are achieving something.

Maintain control in a sensitive way
It is important to avoid arguments and to maintain discussion. This is best done by ensuring that everyone sticks to the point but does not end up scoring points. Some firmness may be needed but this should be tempered by a little latitude. An element of chit-chat helps to keep emotional levels down, as does a touch of humour here and there. Humour is of course a first-class way of defusing a situation which is in danger of becoming adversarial.

The leader should avoid becoming personally involved in any competitive interchanges. One way to avoid this is to put another question to the group to switch them to another subject. There is no reason why, if a subject is becoming something of a hot potato, it cannot be dropped and picked up again later when emotional levels are lower. Whatever you do, don't:

- Shut someone up in a brutal way
- Lose your temper
- Rudely interrupt
- Condemn an expressed opinion as silly, ridiculous, stupid or the like.

End on a dynamic note
A summary of what has been agreed should be made at the end. A

summary of what is still in doubt should also be made. Unresolved matters will need to be dealt with later and it is as well to agree ways and means before breaking up the session. Possibilities include: further fact-finding followed by another meeting; a small sub-group (say two people) to work on it and to report back; or a series of separate discussions between the leader and one or two appropriate people. Whatever the outcome, thank the people for taking part and give recognition to any individual who has been particularly helpful, say, with an idea which everyone supported.

By the way

Avoid using the words 'I' and 'you'. Use instead 'we' and 'us', for example:

> *We* have a problem
>
> There is an opportunity for *us* here
>
> How can *we* best deal with this?
>
> That idea should give *us* some kudos.

The 'I and you' method is divisive and damages the team feeling that the effective leader will strive to maintain. All problems should be 'our' problems – and all successes should be 'our' successes.

Never despair

Developing really effective two-way communication is never easy. Every leader has to learn how to go about it and, as with every learning process, there will be a few failures. Don't give up when things do not work out too well as the only way to achieve proficiency is by practice. As time goes by the hit rate will improve as your team realises what participation means and your use of technique becomes more effective.

A prescription for some useful communication

In 1991 Boots the Chemists decided that it needed some information on the views of employees on a range of subjects. In May 1991 nearly 6,000 employees (about 10 per cent of the payroll) were asked to complete a questionnaire.

Opinions were asked for on levels of satisfaction with jobs, attitudes to customers, equal opportunities, training and, by no means least, communication.

The survey was carried out by MORI to ensure that it was professionally handled and in order to be able to make comparisons with results from other companies which MORI had surveyed. They found for example that 70 per cent of employees expressed satisfaction with their jobs, compared with the service sector norm of 67 per cent.

Particularly interesting and useful information was gathered on why people work for Boots.

The six most frequent reasons were:

Pay	67%
Interesting work	65%
Friendly colleagues	64%
Working for a company which looks after staff	45%
Job security	43%
Staff discount	34%

It is not surprising that pay is the most frequently mentioned reason for working for a company – it is the basic reason that the vast majority of people go to work. However, interesting work and friendly colleagues are rated almost as highly and underline the findings of Hertzberg, Maslow and Likert described in Chapter 2.

The survey also showed that most employees believed that the company cares about its customers (which probably reflects employee attitudes to customer service) but it was not all good news. Only 7 per cent of employees saw the company as an exciting one.

This information and much more was reported back to employees later in the year by means of a well designed and clearly worded booklet titled *Feedback*. The principle of two-way communication was honoured and the booklet included the bad news as well as the good. Most important of all were a number of statements in the brochure showing that the management had taken notice of the results and would take some action.

The booklet included the following messages:

'. . . the results revealed some of the things you feel less happy about. Over the next two years we shall be taking action to make improvements in these areas.'

'Sadly, you don't see us as the most exciting company around! The message is received and understood. Graham Archer, Assured Shopping Co-ordinator, is currently working with managers to look at how we can develop our approach to Quality Teams so that we can make them more interesting and exciting.'

'We are fully committed to Equal Opportunities and are already working on improved awareness of our policies by introducing Equal Opportunity training programmes throughout the company.'

'We won't be sitting back after the survey. We believe that . . . we can improve training still further.'

'. . . there is a need to tell people about the wide career oppportunities which exist within such a big company.'

'Forty-two per cent of you believe that there is not adequate reward for performance . . . our Personnel Department is working with managers to see where we can make more use of performance-related pay . . . .'

This selection of quotations from the brochure shows areas where there is room for improvement and, naturally, this should be the emphasis of the feedback. At the same time, the survey also showed the leaders of the company where they were getting things right.

Such information will be of considerable help in achieving truly effective leadership and the feedback to the employees was, in itself, an opportunity to enhance employee satisfaction and motivation. Gordon Houston, Managing Director, had the last word in the booklet:

> *'It came through in the survey that some of you don't*
> *think we'll take any action after asking for your views. I*
> *assure you that we are already using this valuable*
> *information to work out the best ways to bring together*
> *your wishes and the need to drive the business forward. I*
> *believe that the two go hand in hand.'*

Mr Houston then went on to outline the priorities for management action over the next year.

This case study illustrates how a forward-looking company can communicate with its staff even when they are numbered in terms of thousands and spread over a large number of branches. It also demonstrates how much there is to learn by consulting the people at shop-floor level.

Summary of main points

1 Successful communication requires the use of a number of techniques according to circumstances and just 'telling them' may not mean that real communication has taken place.

2 Careful preparation and skilled transmission are essential requirements and must not be neglected.

3 Preparation for good communication includes:

- Clarification of the purpose
- Thinking through what the other person's viewpoint is likely to be
- Choosing the most advantageous time and place
- Designing a message which is brief and to the point
- Working out a 'structure' for the message.

4 Transmission (or putting the message across effectively) can involve one or more of a number of approaches and methods. Consideration should be given to:

- Visual aids
- The tempo

- Use of technical terms
- Personal enthusiasm
- Written media, for example, notice-boards, memoranda
- The degree of formality.

5 VIPs need to be imaginative about communicating with a large workforce. Passing on a message through a hierarchy of bosses is dangerous but there are alternatives.

6 Effective communication is normally a two-way or multi-way process and the obstacles to this (such as absence of a common objective) need to be removed. Action by the leader may be required to create an environment in which effective communication is possible – before any attempt to communicate is made.

7 Group sessions can be highly effective as a means to communicate. They need careful preparation involving choice of place, an agenda, selection of participants (not always a matter of seniority), and layout. The conduct of the session is crucial in obtaining full and constructive participation and the leader may need to use questions and summaries to keep things going. Control must be sensitive and not inhibit contributions.

8 Case studies from Boots the Chemists and Cummins Engine provide ideas for communications company-wide.

6 Using All the Team Talents

The effective leader, having created a team, will strengthen it and make use of the abilities of all the members by delegating.

Sadly, delegation is a widely misunderstood subject and the technique is much abused and neglected. It does not simply mean giving work to a subordinate, a practice that is often no more than dumping unwanted jobs on to someone else. Real delegation is a more subtle process which can yield substantial benefits to the individuals concerned and to the team as a whole. One of the obstacles to real delegation is the belief sincerely held by many leaders that they have no need to do it. There are also those leaders who believe that their work cannot be delegated. Try this self-check to see whether you need to delegate more.

	YES	NO
1 Do you frequently work longer hours than your staff?	☐	☐
2 Do you spend more than about 30 per cent of your time on detail (as opposed to organising, planning, etc.)?	☐	☐
3 Do you work regular overtime?	☐	☐
4 Do you take work home?	☐	☐

	YES	NO

5 Are your colleagues or subordinates ever held up waiting for you to make a decision? ☐ ☐

6 Do you have difficulty in keeping to deadlines? ☐ ☐

7 Are you doing work which you were doing before you became leader? ☐ ☐

8 Does your work pile up while you are away on holiday? ☐ ☐

9 Have you ever missed some holiday entitlement due to pressure of work? ☐ ☐

10 Is there any work you do which could be done by a junior but you hang on to it because you enjoy it? ☐ ☐

11 Is there any work normally done by your people which comes to a standstill when you are absent for a week or more? ☐ ☐

12 Do you feel, from time to time, that you are dealing mostly with urgent matters rather than important matters? ☐ ☐

If you answered 'No' to every question – and you are quite sure you are right – then you are very probably doing a good job of delegating. Any 'Yes' answers indicate the need to rethink your work and the work of your team members.

You may be one of that large band of managers who fully support the *principle* that delegation is a 'good thing' but find yourself prevented from doing it.

There are a substantial number of obstacles (real and imagined) to delegation and we will examine these in some detail later in this chapter. First, we need some convincing reasons to justify the effort needed for effective delegation. It is not always easy and requires careful planning followed by patient implementation. Why then should we bother?

The benefits of delegation

You, the leader, stand to benefit in the following ways:

You will have more time for the leader's real work
Most of your time should be spent planning ahead, organising work, supporting your people (for example, by training), devising ways to improve things and generally keeping control. You will not be able to do this if every decision depends on you and/or you are up to your neck in day-to-day matters.

Your effectiveness will also be reduced if you are tired by long hours and by work taken home every night. Delegating can make you personally more efficient and may even save you from a nervous breakdown or a sudden heart failure.

Your team will be happier and more productive
You depend on the quality of your team for maintaining or improving your own reputation. Properly conducted delegation can raise the quality of the team in a number of ways. It can be used to improve the challenge and interest in the job of a team member and thereby motivate the person concerned.

Delegation also results in a wider spread of skills throughout the team. This is turn means less dependence on one or two individuals (who may suddenly resign or go sick), and better cover during the holiday season. Any event which results in an increase in a particular kind of work can be better coped with if there is a larger pool of people with the experience to handle it. Above all, it gives you more flexibility and the resources to deal with sudden change or emergencies.

All this adds up to your gaining a reputation as a leader whose team always meets the demands made on it.

Delegation will increase your chances of promotion
There is a widespread notion that bringing on a subordinate is tantamount to signing your own death warrant. The fear that a bright and promising junior will one day ease you out of your job is understandable but not very logical. The fact is that your own promotion will be obstructed if there is no obvious successor for

you. It is not unknown, in boardrooms, to hear a comment such as 'I agree that Blenkinsop is the right person to take over the new subsidiary but we have no one to replace him where he is.' This situation is often met by recruiting someone from outside the company to take over the plum job.

Your own sense of status and self-fulfilment will be improved
Do you really want to carry on with the dreary routine of putting together the sales figures each month or flogging away with the aged debtors' list? Your job will no doubt be more exciting and rewarding if you could spend time on developing your idea for a computerised production planning system or designing a training plan for the next twelve months.

These are just some of the benefits which delegation can bring you.

What about the workers?

Similar benefits await the employee to whom you are delegating. If properly carried out, delegation will enhance the job interest of juniors and improve their market value. Remember that a job which seems boring or burdensome to you may be an exciting new opportunity to someone who has never done it before.

Being given a new responsibility can also motivate by raising the self-esteem of the individual. Similarly, status can be raised and, by no means least, delegation is a form of public recognition. When you pass on a task to someone it is tantamount to saying, 'I think you are capable of doing more, I trust you to do it and recognise your abilities.'

■ If it's so good why don't people do it?

The reasons for not delegating are many and varied but none stands up to serious examination. Some reasons are openly expressed whilst others are hidden. Let's take a look at the more common reasons, openly expressed and all taken from real life:

'I can do the work more quickly myself'
No doubt this is often true. The experienced boss *should* be able to do familiar work more quickly than someone who has never done it before. However if this argument is taken to its logical

conclusion no one would ever hand on work to anyone else, until they retire.

'If I delegate the work, mistakes will be made which we cannot afford'
This is another argument for keeping a task for life. Of course mistakes will be made, in the same way that the boss made them when he or she first tackled the work. The mistakes are all part of the learning process. Proper training, support and intelligent supervision can all minimise the likelihood of errors. The cost of the errors must also be set against the cost of a highly-paid boss doing work which could be done by someone on a lower salary.

'I am constantly under pressure and have no time to teach the job to someone else'
This means two things. First, that the leader has no time for the juniors (who are the future of the company) and therefore no time for the future of the company. Secondly, that the pressure will stay there until a heart failure or a monumental foul-up brings the leader's career to an end.

The vicious circle of too much work and not enough time will continue indefinitely unless the nettle is grasped and the circle broken.

'I spent fifteen years learning the job and now you expect me to hand it over to someone barely out of school'
The man who made this remark was either admitting that he was a very slow learner or had no idea what learning really involves. There are few, if any, jobs which cannot be learned in a matter of weeks or months, given that the necessary basic education is there at the start.

There is a 'learning curve' for every task. The greater part of the job will be learned rapidly in the early stages. As time goes on the learning slows down simply because all the essentials have been covered and the trainee is now picking up odd aspects which are not in the mainstream of the job. These less usual features can, if necessary, be handled by means of *ad hoc* tutorials with the leader. After each one has been dealt with the trainee should know what to do next time and reference to the leader will continue to diminish. It is probably the case that when someone bangs on about how long it has taken to learn the job an attempt is being made to exaggerate its complexity or importance.

'My staff are already overloaded. If I delegate it will break the camel's back.'
This is *sometimes* true but not often. One manager vigorously resisted delegation on the grounds that his staff regularly worked late and could be seen sitting at their desks long after the end of normal business hours. The reason that they did so was not that they were overloaded but because they were afraid to go home until the boss went home! Work was spread out to given them something to do after hours – and everyone hated it. One employee sat doing nothing every evening waiting until it was safe to pack up.

Leaders who use the excuse of overloaded staff have probably not asked their people how *they* feel about delegation. The leader's perception can be, and often is, very wrong. In one case four heads of department each insisted that they could not delegate owing to the existing heavy workloads of their deputies. Three of the four deputies, when consulted, complained that their boss did not delegate enough. As one of them put it, 'He keeps all the interesting work to himself.' This is a good example of the dangers of making assumptions. If in doubt, ask your people how they see it.

'I have to keep in touch with what is going on. If I delegate I will no longer have my finger on the pulse'
This implies that there is no way to keep in touch without being involved in all sorts of detail and is an argument for having no staff at all! Good communication by means of review meetings and other forms of feedback should be quite enough to keep the leader informed. As often as not being too closely involved actually clouds the picture. The wood can be better seen from a distance rather than from among the trees.

'I have no suitable staff to whom I can delegate'
This statement is a confession of managerial incompetence. It means that the leader has made mistakes in recruiting the wrong people or in failing to train them. In addition he or she is perpetuating the situation by not giving them the experience they need and, in effect, by doing their work for them.

'I have tried it before and it did not work'
Failure is almost always the result of not delegating properly. It is worth repeating that delegation is not a quick and easy operation. It requires careful planning and execution – as you will see later in this chapter.

The unspoken reasons

There are bosses, usually promoted beyond their level of competence, who have reasons for not delegating which they are not readily willing to admit. These reasons include:

1 A belief that handing over work will diminish the leader's authority and he or she will lose control.

2 A fear of being regarded as non-essential if not seen to be beavering away behind mountains of files or whatever.

3 Uncertainty about what the scope and responsibilities of the job are. People who are unsure about the content of their jobs cannot delegate properly.

4 Feeling more comfortable when dealing with relatively simple routine duties rather than tackling the more demanding role of a true leader.

Anyone burdened by one or more of these obstacles has a serious problem and needs to consider carefully the underlying attitudes. For example, a fear that delegation will reduce authority suggests a lack of self-confidence. In fact, sound delegation can serve to increase authority by providing more time for the things on which real authority is based.

Likewise, a fear of being thought to be non-essential also suggests a poor level of self-confidence (and maybe self-esteem) and questions the values and culture of the organisation.

Uncertainty about your job and what its scope really is suggests that your own boss is performing badly as a leader and also that you are not communicating effectively with him or her.

Hiding away behind the routine work is an abdication of responsibility and may also suggest that you have not prepared yourself for your true role. Sticking to the old, familiar, technical work will also reduce your authority: you are making yourself no different from your people.

These are some of the obstacles to delegation which the would-be effective leader must overcome. There is another side to the coin.

The delegatee's problems

Not everyone is waiting with enthusiasm and bated breath for work to be delegated to them. Some, despite being capable of doing the work, will be discouraged by a number of fears:

Fear of making mistakes

This is how the employee is likely to describe the fear but in reality the fear is of the consequence of those mistakes. If the employee has any reason to believe that mistakes will result in punishment then he or she will not want to risk it.

Lack of information or skill

Unless the employee is reassured that adequate training will be given he or she will naturally see the delegated work as a burden to be avoided.

Lack of incentive

The leader must make it clear that there is something in it for the delegatee. The benefits, which must be genuine, will need to be pointed out. It is a common mistake to assume that the employee can see the benefits as clearly as the boss can. In any case the employee's viewpoint and perception will, at least at the outset, be different.

It's up to you to remove the obstacles

Many of the obstacles are in the minds of leaders who, for one reason or another, are reluctant to delegate. These obstacles can be removed by thinking it through carefully and adding up the benefits. There is little doubt that really effective leadership is impossible without a high degree of delegation.

The obstacles in the minds of reluctant delegatees can also only be removed by the leader who must demonstrate that the employees' fears will not be translated into reality.

This brings us to the ways and means to go about delegating.

The delegation process

Delegation is a process and not an event. Some would argue that once the process starts it never really ends, being an activity which is self-perpetuating. In a well-led team this is almost certainly true with delegation being such a normal part of a lively and changing scene that it goes on almost automatically. However it all starts with the leader. This is what you need to do.

1 List all the work that you do which you, *and only you*, must do.

You may find this list to be a short one. It might include such items as carrying out appraisal interviews, disciplinary matters, salary awards and reporting progress to the managing director.

Most of what you do will not have an element of confidentiality or be particularly 'sensitive'.

2 Now list all the work not on the first list which takes up a lot of your time.

To do this accurately keep a log of your activities for a few days to obtain a clear picture of how your time is used. Such a log often produces some results which are surprising. Our subjective impressions of what we spend our time on are frequently wildly inaccurate as in the case of the manager who reckoned he spent about 2 per cent of his time reading incoming mail. In fact he read all his department's incoming mail ('to keep a finger on the pulse') and this never took less than an hour each morning. This amounted to over 12½ per cent of his time *and* he held up his team who could not get on with their jobs until he passed the mail to them.

3 Now rank the non-sensitive work you do in descending order of the amount of time required.

This gives you the first guidelines for work which can be most usefully delegated *in order to reduce your own time pressures.*

4 Next look at each item on your list of work and decide if there is anything which can be done better by one of your team. You might find it difficult to accept that something which you do could be done more effectively by one of your people but it is not uncommon to find bosses doing work in which their subordinates are more expert.

Put a tick against any work which fits this category.

5 Look at the list again. Is there anything which, if learned and done by someone else would strengthen the team? For example, is there any item of work which only you do and which comes to a halt whenever you are absent? Is there an opportunity to get something done more quickly (i.e., deadlines are more likely to be met) if someone other than yourself can also do it?

Anything within this category should be ticked.

6 Now take a final look at the list. Is there any work which is frequently characterised by its urgency but is not especially important? If so, place a tick against that item.

You will now have a list of your work which you might delegate with the ticks indicating the most promising items. Some tasks may have two or more ticks indicating that delegating them will result in particular advantage.

Be brave and imaginative

Have another look at your list. Have you really tried hard to be objective and realistic? In particular, go back to the tasks which you believed could not be delegated. Are you sure? One leader had included amongst his 'must do' list the preparation of his departmental monthly report. This report, which his boss insisted on receiving, was something of a burden. It involved a regular month-end scramble involving much tiresome chasing of section heads for facts and figures. This was followed by analysis of the figures and drawing conclusions.

After some thought the manager called his section heads together and proposed that they should take turns in writing the report. The section heads accepted the idea with enthusiasm. It was agreed that the manager would remain accountable for the quality and timeliness of the report and, as far as was necessary, help the section head preparing it.

The benefits which resulted were:

- A new area of interest for the section heads
- Reduced pressure on the manager
- The report no longer depended on the presence of the manager
- The section heads became more aware of the importance of having their own facts and figures available at month-end
- An increased sense of team responsibility for work which had to be done.

Another benefit which arose was a new and more effective means of analysing some of the figures. One of the section heads who had a degree in mathematics suggested some statistical techniques which the manager was not aware of.

These were explained to the manager and the other section heads and used for future reports. The result was utilisation of a previously unused skill present in the team and the learning of that skill by other team members.

■ To whom should you delegate?

Choosing the people to whom you might delegate is as important as choosing the work involved. A mismatch can result in wasted opportunities or even a disaster. The key is to look at the prospects from the employee's point of view, for example:

- Which employees would benefit from learning new skills?
- Are there any employees who would be able to perform more effectively if responsibility were delegated? For example, someone who could act on the spot more

rapidly if he or she did not have to wait for your decision or instruction.

- Is there someone who is a likely candidate for promotion in the future who could be more rapidly developed?

- Is there any employee who has indicated a desire for more responsibility (or workload)?

- Are there any skills or qualifications not being fully utilised? Someone may, for example, have completed a training course but has not had the opportunity to use the knowledge gained. This can be particularly important. People who have put in the effort to gain skills or pass an examination are likely to look elsewhere for a chance to use them if you do not provide the opportunity.

- Is there a chance to even out workloads, i.e., is there someone you suspect may be underemployed?

In general look for opportunities to add interest and challenge. Look for people who can be further developed and 'grown'. Not least, look for ways to give the employee greater control over his or her own work and more opportunity to make decisions. These are the things which will motivate and improve productivity. And anything which takes the pressure off you will add to the likelihood that you will perform more effectively as a leader.

You will now have a tentative list of people with some work which might be delegated to them. Next comes another bout of careful thinking.

■ *What will the delegation entail?*

You must avoid dumping work on people. Just handing it over and telling them to get on with it is a sure recipe for disaster for the individual, for the team and for you.

The employee has a right to expect adequate training for the new work and enough time to learn before taking on the responsibility involved. As a preliminary to discussing the delegation with the employee work out a simple plan like this:

DELEGATION PLAN – MARY SMITH		
OBJECTIVE: To enable Mary Smith to take over the despatch department by 1 January		
Work to be delegated	*Training required*	*Target date for handover*
1. Vehicle scheduling	Two weeks with transport manager	1 October
2. Warehouse space allocation	One week in warehouse	1 November
3. Preparation of despatch schedule	Despatch computer system	1 December
4. Leading despatch team	Team leader course	1 January

This plan may not at this stage be complete in every detail but should be enough to form a basis for discussion.

How does the employee feel about it?

The proposed delegation and the outline plan can now be put to the employee concerned. The idea may be very welcome to the employee but be prepared for him or her to have some reservations. The outline plan should dispel any fears of having to take on new work without adequate preparation but there could still be some worries lurking about. You must be ready to *listen* to what the employee says and either to offer the necessary assurances or be prepared to go back to the drawing-board. You can and should offer encouragement but don't force the issue.

The employee may need time to think the proposals over and this time should be given.

If you know your people well (which you should) and they trust you any obstacles will probably be readily overcome and you can proceed to the next step which is to agree the plan.

■ Firming up the delegation plan

The employee must be involved in the details of the plan you have drawn up. It is likely that he or she will have some ideas and opinions about content and timing and these should be taken into account. The commitment of the employee is vital and will be strengthened by having an influence on events. Apart from that the employee is likely to be more aware of what it is he or she may have to learn and may have some good ideas as to how to go about it.

Once the plan is agreed with the employee you will need to discuss it with other people involved, in particular anyone who is to help with the training. When all the key players are in the picture you will need to communicate it more widely.

Letting everyone know

First and foremost you must tell your team what is going on and why. You may need to have individual sessions with individual people and then inform the whole team at the next briefing session.

Co-operation (or at least an awareness of who will be doing what in future) may be required from other departments than your own and they too should be informed. If not, people will rightly continue to regard you as the person doing the work and will ignore the person to whom you have delegated.

This can also involve customers and suppliers who are used to dealing with you. It may be highly desirable to introduce the new person to them. This makes them feel valued and involved and can reduce any antipathy to dealing with a new contact, who would otherwise be just a name.

■ Implementing the delegation plan

No amount of careful planning and preparation will result in anything useful if implementation is badly handled.

The first rule is 'Stick to the plan come hell or high water'.

Your employee (it is to be hoped looking forward with enthusiasm to the new tasks) will be well and truly demotivated if you fail to start as arranged or do not keep up the programme once started. You will almost certainly face a time problem if you need to teach the work and will be tempted to postpone a session or two when an urgent matter comes along. To some extent this may be handled if you can delegate the teaching to someone else who will step in if you really cannot do it yourself. However this could be a poor substitute as far as the trainee is concerned.

If you are the person to do the teaching there is a way to help ensure that you do it yourself and that you do it as arranged.

On-job-training (the time beater)

Let's be quite clear about one thing. On-job-training (OJT) is not 'sitting next to Nellie'. This is probably the worst type of 'training' ever devised and usually results in very little progress, unless Nellie is a trained trainer and has a clear incentive to teach the person concerned. True OJT is a methodical approach based on breaking down the subject to be learned into digestible chunks.

It works like this:

1 Define the broad job to be learned, let's say, processing incoming sales orders.

2 Break down the job into its various parts, for example:

- Checking the order – quantities, product codes, etc.
- Checking stock levels against the order
- Preparing despatch instructions
- Preparing production orders when stock is not available
- Preparing documentation for delivery and billing.

There may be more to the job than this but five parts will suffice for illustration.

3 Take each part of the job is turn and estimate how long it will take to teach it:

- Checking the order   –   20 minutes
- Checking stock levels   –   15 minutes
- Preparing despatch instructions   –   30 minutes
- Preparing production orders   –   30 minutes
- Preparing documentation   –   25 minutes.

These times will be those required to cover the basic information, not to make the trainee an expert. That will come from practice over some weeks.

4 Now, with the involvement of the trainee, draw up a training programme which includes time for supervised practice and for review of progress. The training programme will look like this:

TRAINING PROGRAMME – BILL BROWN

Date	Time	Subject	Trainer
1.6.93	9.30–9.50	Order checking	B. Smith
2.6.93	All day	Practice	,,
3.6.93	9.30–9.45	Review of Progress	,,
	9.45–5.00	Practice	,,
4.6.93	9.30–9.45	Checking stock levels	,,
	9.45–5.00	Practice	,,
5.6.93	9.30–10.00	Despatch instructions	A. Green
	10.00–5.00	Practice	,,
8.6.93	9.30–10.00	Review of progress	B. Smith

A programme such as this has the following advantages:

1 The actual time spent teaching is short. This makes it a practical proposition for busy leaders to find the time, especially if the teaching session is started at the same time each day and can be planned for. A routine can be developed in which, for example, the trainer can have someone else taking his or her telephone calls or otherwise holding the fort.

2 The time spent learning is short. This means that the trainee will not become exhausted and will find each chunk more digestible.

3 The trainee can begin to take over the work at an early stage.

If, as in the example, the first part of the training is followed by actually doing it then the benefits to all concerned are gained without delay.

4 The chances of serious errors are reduced by the gradual nature of the process, a feature which can give confidence to a nervous trainee.

5 Both trainer and trainee know what is expected of them and have a yardstick by which to measure progress.

The training programme must be followed punctiliously and in a disciplined way but, like any plan of action, can be amended if an advantage can be seen. If, for example, the trainee finds a particular subject difficult then the programme could be changed to repeat the session or perhaps allow more time for practice. Or you might realise that adding another task to the job being delegated would be a good idea and so slot in an extra session to cater for it.

The OJT programme should guide you to a successful outcome but there are a few traps to be wary of.

Some do's and don'ts of delegation

Do allow ample time for the training and exercise patience. What may seem easy to you may be unfamiliar and difficult to the employee.

Do let the employee get on with it. Don't interfere every five minutes fussing about what is being done. This destroys confidence and will make the employee think you don't really want to delegate the work. At the same time:

Do make yourself available to help if real difficulties come along.

Don't get upset if the employee makes a mistake. This is all part of the learning process and may be caused by poor teaching on your part!

Don't insist that the employee does the work exactly how you would do it. We all have different ways of doing things and what works well with one person may not work well with another. Allow some latitude and keep your mind open to the possibility that the employee may have found a way to do the job which is better than the way you did it!

Do watch out for the occasional person who finds it easier to ask you how to do the job rather than having a serious go at it. This often indicates a lack of confidence and you may have to offer reassurance.

Do allow for regular follow-up sessions to be held after the training programme is completed. These can become less frequent as time goes on and should be stopped as soon as the employee is fully in control.

Do make it clear what the purpose of the work is, the standards required and any deadlines. Anything you forget to mention may not be obvious to the employee.

Don't fail to delegate any authority which should go along with the responsibility.

Do reward success and effort at least by recognition.

It's not just work you must think about

One of the most valuable forms of delegation does not involve handing over tasks as such. Monitoring and decision taking can also be delegated and ideally the responsibility for these should be placed at the lowest possible level. It is more effective if the person doing the job checks progress against agreed targets and standards and, without involving the leader, takes any necessary remedial action. If action is only taken by the leader (after the leader has totted up the facts and figures) the result will be unsatisfactory in the following ways:

1 There will be a delay between an unfavourable trend developing and action taken to remedy it.

2 The person doing the job will not feel wholly responsible for the work.

3 If the leader does not check then no one will.

4 The checking takes up the leader's time.

If your people are properly trained then trust them to keep things under control themselves – and tell them that you trust them.

Summary of main points

1 Delegation is a powerful but much neglected and often misunderstood weapon in the effective leader's armoury.

2 The benefits of delegation extend to the leader who delegates, the delegatee and the team. They include:

- More time for the leader to concentrate on the important matters rather than the urgent ones
- Individuals become more productive
- Delegation can be a powerful motivator
- Delegation improves the leader's chances of promotion
- Development of up and coming people.

3 There are some real (and imagined) obstacles to delegation which may face the leader. Examples include the familiar 'I can do it more quickly myself' argument and the fear that giving the work to a less experienced person will result in mistakes being made.

None of these arguments stands up to serious examination and all such obstacles can be overcome.

4 There are often unspoken reasons for not delegating including:

- A fear that handing over work will diminish the leader's authority
- A fear of appearing to be non-essential
- A preference for the more comfortable option of keeping busy all day on relatively simple and routine work.

5 The delegatee can also have problems and fears which the leader must deal with. They include:

- Fear of making mistakes – and of getting into trouble as a result
- Lack of incentive to take over new work
- Lack of information or skill.

6 Delegation is a process not an event. It requires an analysis of the leader's work and the skills, aspirations and potential of team members. This analysis will lead to the potentially most profitable opportunities and helps avoid 'dumping'.

7 Leaders need to be brave and imaginative and not be restricted by false notions of 'confidentiality' or 'political' considerations.

8 A delegation plan (however simple) is required. This plan, worked out and agreed with the delegatee, should be designed to achieve a clear objective.

9 Training is almost always a prerequisite of good delegation. On-job-training (*not* sitting next to Nellie) is a useful way to overcome the old problem of finding the time to train.

10 The delegation plan must be communicated to all who may be affected by it including other departments and, where appropriate, people outside the organisation.

11 Implementation must be carefully handled with patience and understanding of the viewpoint of the person learning the work.

There are a number of do's and don'ts to keep in mind.

12 It's not just jobs which can be delegated. Pushing the responsibility for monitoring quality and quantity of work (and generally controlling work) down to the lowest possible level will pay dividends.

7 Finding the Right People

Clearly your success as a leader will depend heavily on the quality of the people in your team. The quality can be improved by your own actions such as the training you give them and the general development and encouragement they receive.

However, there are limits. Someone with an I.Q. of 100 cannot be turned into an Einstein and someone with a serious personality defect might find co-operation with colleagues very difficult. It follows that selecting the people for your team is a vital skill and there are some techniques you can learn and put into practice. Fortunately most of it boils down to common sense applied with a conscious awareness of the things which really matter.

The first question which you should ask yourself is:

■ Do I need to recruit at all?

There is a natural knee-jerk reaction to someone's departure – find a replacement. Before doing so pause and think about it.

Someone's resignation or retirement is an ideal opportunity to take stock of the situation in two ways:

1 Do I need to replace the leaver?

2 Do I need the same kind of person again?

The vacancy may be more apparent than real. For example, the departure may provide the opportunity for beneficial changes such as:

Mechanising the work
A computer system might, for example, replace some routine clerical work. It is often the case that computerisation would have been resisted by the former incumbent but his or her disappearance from the scene clears the way for change.

Sharing the work among the remaining people
This might be welcome as a means of adding interest to jobs, improving someone's sense of status or, by concentrating work in fewer hands, improving accuracy and control.

Sub-contracting the work to an outside agency
Times change and so do costs. What may have been cost-effective to do in-house a few years ago may now be done more cheaply by an outside specialist. Payroll preparation is an example of work which often falls into this category.

A further fundamental question which should be asked and seriously thought about is, 'Do we need to continue doing the work?' This is not so silly a question as it may seem. Work which is virtually obsolete can go on simply because someone does it and its usefulness is not questioned. In one case a senior clerk refused to accept a transfer to a new company location and preferred to take early retirement. At first this was regarded as a mini-disaster until his work was seriously examined. It was eventually realised that much of his time had been taken up with unnecessary checking and recording and, with a little reorganising of the office systems, he need not be replaced. This kind of result can be found at senior levels too, including the board-level executive who was responsible for 'Export Sales Liaison'. This turned out to be nothing worth keeping and after the executive's retirement was quietly dropped.

Despite the various possibilities you may decide that the vacancy must be filled and this is how to do it.

Starting the search

Knowing what you really want is more than half the battle and a review of the job description is the first essential step. Job descriptions are often mistakenly regarded as a boring and time-wasting piece of bureaucracy. They are in fact a sound means to analyse a job, what it should involve and what it should not. The job description also helps to ensure that the employee knows what is expected of him or her and this has a motivating effect.

It is important to realise that it is the *job* which is being defined and not the person doing it. The job description may also not match up with the job *as it is or has been done* and this is where the description becomes doubly useful if you have a vacancy. Thinking it through and writing it up will force you to review what the role really should be and this in turn will form a basis for finding the person you want.

■ *What should the job description look like?*

Keep the description as brief and to the point as possible. Ideally it will all appear on one page and look something like this:

JOB DESCRIPTION

Job title: Laboratory technician

Responsibilities: Carrying out routine chemical testing under the control of the laboratory supervisor

Duties:

1   To receive and record samples for testing

2   To carry out tests for toxicity and volatility

3   To complete reports showing the results of each test including correlation co-efficients as appropriate

4   To apply sampling to bulk products and report results showing statistical validity

5   To check and maintain safety measures in the laboratory

6   To check and maintain laboratory equipment to standards laid down from time to time

---

From the recruitment angle the job description starts to point to the type of person you will need.

The laboratory technician required to do the job described will need to be:

- Methodical and able to deal with detail
- Have technical expertise, for example, in toxicity testing
- Be able to work out co-efficients and cope with other mathematical and statistical processes
- Understand safety matters as applied to laboratory conditions and to be able to spot inadequacies in equipment.

The description may emphasise that the person doing the job will be working alone or at least will not share tasks with colleagues. If this is so then you will need someone who is happy to work in isolation.

The job description can, by this simple analysis, lead to a profile of the sort of person most suited to the job. Normally the level of technical knowledge is fairly easy to specify and is evidenced by basic qualifications combined with relevant experience. Take care to add to the profile attributes such as:

- Tact and calmness (for example, if likely to be faced with customer complaints)
- A friendly and courteous manner (for example, if dealing with members of the public)
- Good oral communication skills (for example, a solicitor)

Building up this fairly detailed picture is an exercise which may take you some time and effort but it pays. You will have to expend much more time and effort in resolving the problems which can arise if the wrong type of person is sought and recruited.

Some traps to avoid

Discrimination on the grounds of sex and race is illegal in many countries and is in any case damaging. It may not be appropriate for a woman to be employed as an attendant in a men's lavatory (although this works perfectly well in France) but to reduce by discrimination your chances of finding the right person is self-defeating.

One of the most common mistakes is to discriminate on the grounds of age. You may have age limitations because of a need for the recruit to 'fit in' (a subject dealt with later) but the almost automatic ceiling of thirty-five to forty years which appears in advertisements is ridiculous. The justification for excluding older people is commonly stated as the need for energy and drive. Certainly younger people can offer these attributes but how does the justification stand up when it is made by a fifty-five-year-old personnel director or a sixty-year-old managing director? Would they admit to being over the hill and useless?

Even if an older person has slowed down a bit this can be more than balanced by the experience of that person and the likelihood that he or she will be more consistent and stable. There are examples of some imaginative and successful thinking to be found in the retail world. A policy of employing older (including retired) people to do humdrum work in the branches of certain large companies has paid off. The older employees are happy to undertake unexciting but unstressful work and employers have experienced low staff turnover rates, low absenteeism and generally all-round high levels of reliability.

Too much for too little

Watch out also for the trap of asking for more qualifications than are needed. A company in London adopted the policy of only recruiting 'A'-level people for one of its departments. The manager believed that work quality would improve but the result was quite the reverse. The 'A'-level youngsters who came into the department expected work which would stretch and challenge them. They found instead routine work which was too easy for them and boring. After wasting a lot of money as a result of a series of early resignations it was realised that people with lower expectations and less ability would be happier and do the job better.

Look at the job from the worker's point of view and decide which horse is best for the course.

The question of fitting in

It takes only one misfit to wreck a whole team.

Every group of people whether it be a team of workers or, say, a tennis club, football team or a school class will, in time, develop its own culture. There will be norms of behaviour, language and even dress which will identify the group. There will also be an in-built wariness of newcomers who are introduced into the group and, in some cases, open hostility. It is probably true that the stronger the sense of team pride and loyalty the greater the difficulty in fully integrating a newcomer.

This means that at least as much attention must be paid to finding someone who will be acceptable to the team and become a true member of it as to the academic or technical qualifications and experience required. The profile should include the personal attributes which are likely to encourage assimilation into the team. These are not easy to identify and some may be so subtle as to be virtually impossible to describe. However, clues can be obtained by looking at the broad characteristics of the existing team members. These might include such features as:

- Enjoyment of a joke, including some leg-pulling
- Interest in sports or other leisure interests
- Broadly 'middle-class' background
- Absence of aversion to alcohol or smoking
- Absence of strong political views – or at least an unwillingness to express them
- Support for organised company activities such as the social club, cricket team and charity fund raising.

Finding someone who exactly matches these characteristics may be next to impossible but awareness of them may prevent you from employing someone whose ideas are positively inimical. A very serious-minded person with very strong political views and who is a campaigner to ban tobacco and alcohol is likely to clash with a team having the broad characteristics listed above.

The level of success in correctly listing the type of characteristics to look for will depend heavily on your personal judgement and your knowledge of the people in your team. Fortunately, as will be seen, the job can be made easier by involving your people in the selection process.

Having prepared the job description and the consequent person profile you will be ready to start the search.

The body hunt

The first place to look is inside your own company. You may well have the right person for the job sitting there waiting for an opportunity.

The advantages of recruiting from within include:

- *You know the person and his or her qualities*
  This substantially reduces the chances of a misfit.

- *You will save money*
  There will be no advertising or other recruitment costs unless, of course, the person recruited must in turn be replaced by finding an outsider.

- *Internal recruitment can be motivating*
- It demonstrates that opportunities will be offered to existing staff.

- *Training costs are normally lower*
  The insider will require less induction and will probably have some (or even all) of the basic knowledge of products, etc., which is required.

The major disadvantage, which can be most marked at a senior level, is that 'new blood' is not being brought into the business. It is often highly desirable to bring in outsiders in order to introduce new thinking and attitudes; it is sometimes essential to recruit externally to acquire technical skills which are lacking. However, a good look at the people already on the payroll should be your first step.

If there are no suitable people then the outside world must be explored but this can be done by the people you already have as an alternative to the more traditional methods.

■ Who knows whom?

Your existing staff will know what sort of people will fit in to the culture of your company and your team. They may know people of the right type with appropriate skills and experience whom they can recommend and approach.

Finding someone by this method offers advantages:

- Advertising and other search costs are saved. Some companies offer a payment to employees who find someone for a vacancy but the cost of this is normally a good deal less than using the traditional methods. The payment to an employee is, at least in the short term, a motivator.

- An employee is unlikely to recommend someone who is not suitable as he or she will have to live with the results of their actions.

- The recruit is more likely to be acceptable to the team if supported by an existing team member. This often means faster integration of the newcomer.

If these 'internal' methods fail then there is a choice of two main options: using an agency or advertising.

■ Using an agency

There are some very good agencies – and some very bad ones. If you have no experience of using an agency it will pay you to shop around with care. It may help you to take the following precautions.

- Ask for and take up references. A reputable agency should be willing to give you the names of regular clients to whom you can refer.

- Check the charges. These can range from 10 per cent to 35 per cent of the first year's salary of the recruit.

- Find out exactly what the agency will do for their fee. Some will merely advertise and pass on the replies to you to sort out. Others will carry out initial interviews and present you with a shortlist. Some will offer 'extras' such as psychological tests. These should be treated with caution as they add to the cost but are not universally regarded as reliable.

Basically, you get what you pay for but not everything may be worth paying for.

■ *Advertising*

The many pages of job ads in the local and national newspapers indicate the popularity of this method. Results can be very variable depending on how you go about it and, since advertising is costly, care is needed.

The two most critical decisions are where to advertise and what to say.

Choosing the medium

Deciding where to place your advertisement depends on what the type of person you are looking for will read, not necessarily what *you* are likely to read. Similarly, avoid the mistake of choosing a prestige journal (thinking it will be good for your company image) if it is not likely to reach the market you are aiming at.

A local newspaper may be a better bet than a national one (and a lot cheaper) and there may be particular trade or professional magazines which will pinpoint your targets more accurately.

What to say

Some advertisers for employees seem to forget the purpose of the advertisement. Its primary function is to communicate effectively with a particular type of person and whilst some information on your company is required a lengthy essay on how marvellous you are is rarely necessary.

Your advertisement should say:

1. Who you are
Give the name of your company and a *brief* description of your business. For example, 'We are print manufacturers employing about ninety people at a modern factory on a Croydon trading estate.' This tells the reader what your company does, its size and

location. You also mention your modern factory which dispels any fears that you employ people in a down-at-heel Dickensian sweatshop.

2. The job to be done

This is where your carefully prepared job description pays off once again. The main items of your description can be placed in your advertisement to make clear to readers the nature of the work to be done. If you fail to do this you will waste time and money dealing with applications from unsuitable people.

Avoid very general terms such as 'clerk', or 'operator'. These can mean almost anything within a broad context and do not describe the real nature of the work to be done. Something fairly specific is required, for example, 'Milling machine operator to work on precision mouldings in both steel and non-ferrous metals'; or 'Cost clerk to assist the chief estimator in preparing tenders for major construction schemes'.

Such descriptions tell readers enough about the job to be able to decide if it is likely to appeal to them and whether they have the necessary skills to do it.

Something else to avoid is the use of names for jobs which are peculiar to your own company. A company which advertised for 'client executives' received many replies from salespeople. The company was not looking for salespeople at all and the title of the job meant (internally) something entirely different.

3. The type of person you are seeking

This is where the person profile comes in. List the key requirements in the way of skills and experience. Some people find it helpful to state which are essential and which are desirable attributes, thus perhaps painting a clearer picture of the person sought without excluding those who are not ideal but come close.

4. The rewards and other conditions

Some advertisers are remarkably coy about salaries. Some say nothing at all about what they are prepared to pay whilst others use vague terms such as 'negotiable' or 'appropriate to the importance of the position'. This last expression is as pompous as '*highly* negotiable' is ridiculous. The salary should be mentioned if only to avoid wasting time on people who already earn more or would not change jobs for the amount you are prepared to pay. In addition there are many people who will disregard an advertisement which does not mention salary as it seems that the company has something to hide.

Other goodies such as holiday entitlement, pension scheme, staff discount and subsidised meals should also be briefly but clearly mentioned.

The invitation to apply

Please make it easy for people to apply for the job. It also pays to be friendly.

This sort of wording will not encourage applications:

> '*Applications, accompanied by a full* curriculum vitae *must be received at this office no later than 10 January. Your application must include a statement, in your own handwriting, showing how you meet the requirements of the position.*'

This kind of demand is usually followed by sending every applicant a multi-page application form with questions that the *c.v.* has already answered plus a number of others with no apparent relevance. It is at this stage that more applicants get fed up and pull out. If you *must* have an application form at least make it simple and avoid using it as a duplication of a *c.v.*

A more productive approach is along these lines:

> '*If this job appeals to you send us a brief note or, if more convenient, call us on 071–699 0011. We will send you a short application form. Alternatively, if you have a* c.v. *just send us a copy.*'

Sorting out the applications

An efficient sorting process is needed to deal with the applications received, if only to ensure that every applicant is responded to promptly. There are some companies who do themselves no good at all by ignoring unwanted applicants altogether. These are often the same companies who are slow in responding to the attractive applicants. A good leader will see that this does not happen as it damages the company in the following ways:

- An impression of discourtesy at best and massive arrogance at worst is given to a number of people. Every company needs friends and creating enemies makes no sense.

- Delays can mean the loss of potentially good people who might find an alternative job in the meantime. The best applicant could end up with your main competitor.

- The misery caused by delays should not be underestimated. The applicant may be looking eagerly for the postman each morning and as each day passes without any news, anxiety will mount. This also can create enemies.

Make sure that you have a system ready for prompt action. You may, for example, receive a number of applications from obviously unsuitable people. These should be quickly weeded out and sent a *friendly* rejection letter which includes your thanks for their time and trouble and wishing them well for the future.

The remaining applicants will probably need some further sifting and a formal method for doing so will encourage objectivity. Some companies find a rating system very helpful. This involves awarding points against those parts of the person profile which can be estimated from the *c.v.* or application form. For example:

	Score out of 10
Formal qualifications	10
Industry experience	8
Sales experience	8
Knowledge of German	5
Sales team leading	1
	32

This method produces better results than gaining a general impression from the application forms or *curriculum vitae*.

Those who score least well or applicants whose score on an essential item is too low to be acceptable will now be eliminated and a rejection letter can be sent to them *promptly*.

The remainder will probably form your shortlist for an interview. Those applicants should now be contacted to arrange an interview date *convenient to them*. They should also be sent some further information about your company. This might include your products brochure, annual report and any other literature which will help the applicant to form a view of your company. This is likely to make any subsequent interview more productive and enhances the applicant's ability to judge whether he or she is suited to the job. Assessing suitability is the role and responsibility of both parties, not just the employer.

Dealing with the shortlist: interviews

Even if you favour psychological testing it will be almost certain that at some stage an interview will take place and your decision will depend heavily on it.

The purpose of the interview should be clear in order to ensure that the interviewer's attitude is the right one. Too many interviewers go about the job looking for reasons to reject and, by a process of elimination, find the applicant with least faults. This is the wrong way round. The search should be for the *positive* attributes which the candidate brings which best meet your needs.

Other common faults in interviewing include:

- Regarding the interview as a battle of wits between applicant and interviewer
- Using cross-examination methods more suitable to an obviously devious witness in a high court trial
- Pressurising the applicant 'to see what he or she is made of'
- Talking too much and listening too little. Some interviewers talk at length and by doing so give the applicant the 'right' answers to any subsequent questions
- Showing off, for example, by boasting about the interviewer's seniority and importance (any intelligent applicant will switch off as soon as this starts)

- Failure to bone up on the applicant's details and to have some relevant and worthwhile questions ready.

Clearly the way in which the interview is conducted is of prime importance and poor interviewing can result in poor recruitment. The right atmosphere – friendly, relaxed, constructive – is essential. This atmosphere can be created well before you meet the applicant.

■ *Setting it up*

Think about the administration which will help to ensure a productive interview. Put yourself in the applicant's shoes and remove any obstacles which he or she may face.

The applicant may have problems in getting to you and may be worried about being late. Send the applicant some information on how to find you, for example:

- A map of your immediate area
- Suggested routes
- Parking facilities
- Bus routes
- Nearest railway station.

You may occupy a large building or a sprawling factory site. Tell the applicant which entrance, floor or building to go to.

There is nothing more unsettling for an applicant than getting lost or turning up at the wrong building. One applicant for a job was told to report at 'the High Street' branch. She did so, not knowing that there were *two* branches in the High Street. She was sent from one to the other and back again before the problem was sorted out. By this time she was late and (unjustly) blamed herself for it. The consequences included a rushed interview after which she was given a job for which she was not suitable.

A welcome smile

Make sure that the arriving applicant is well received. Give the receptionist the name of the person, time of arrival and to whom he or she should be conducted. A cup of coffee may be welcome to an applicant who has travelled a long way and so is an indication of where to find a lavatory. There are many people too nervous to ask for the use of a lavatory and it is not unknown for school leavers and other less than confident people to sit through an interview with a painful bladder.

Other steps to take include:

Dealing with the applicant promptly
Apart from the discourtesy of keeping them waiting, any time spent sitting in a reception area is time for anxiety to increase. It is not good enough that an applicant who has turned up at the agreed time to be told that, 'Mr Bloggs is in a meeting,' or, as happened in one case, 'Mr So-and-so has gone to lunch'! The applicant is important to you and should be treated as such.

Preparing the place
A quiet, comfortable room is needed for an interview. Ideally the interviewer and the applicant will be comfortably and equally seated without a desk between them. The desk is a psychological barrier as well as a physical one and tends to block easy communication. Never make the applicant feel inferior.

Prepare your questions and refresh your memory on the applicant's details
In addition have the job description handy with a copy for the applicant along with anything else (an organisation chart?) which will help the applicant to assess accurately the nature of the job on offer.

■ The interview – who should conduct it?

Without doubt the team leader should choose the people for his or her team and this normally means carrying out the interviews. The practice in some companies where people are selected by more senior people or by a personnel manager is wholly wrong and cannot be justified by saying that team leaders are not trained in selection techniques. They should be so trained.

The fact is that the team leader is responsible and accountable for the performance of his or her team and if someone else chooses the people he or she has a cast-iron excuse for a failure. It can also be a very valid excuse as someone remote from the team must have less familiarity with its culture and needs.

The leader can, however, involve others in the selection process. Those others are existing members of the team.

The really tricky part of the selection process is in deciding if an individual will fit in. If there is even a slight mismatch integration may not be successful in the face of any reserve or suspicion of the newcomer felt by existing members. The chance of a mismatch can be reduced by participation of all or some of the team members.

This is how one leader of a small team of specialists did it:

> 'I would sift out the applications myself and eliminate the obviously unsuitable people. I would try to get the remainder down to about a dozen who had the right technical background and generally seemed to fit the bill.
>
> I would then ask one or two of my team colleagues to help me in selecting a shortlist of two or three for interview. This selection would be largely based on the experience and know-how of the candidates as described in their applications. We would then arrange interviews to take place in the late afternoon. I would conduct the interview myself with a team member present and then the whole team would take the candidate for a drink in the local pub. I never found a candidate who objected to this and the great advantage was that everyone could meet the candidate and form an opinion. We could see if he would mesh with us and he could see if he liked us.
>
> We never had more than eight people in the team so it was easy to arrange. The great thing is that it worked and we never had a failure.'

After the interview – what next?

If any applicants are clearly unsuitable let them know without delay. They may have other applications in the pipeline or even an offer or two and they will not want to be kept waiting for your decision.

You may have a preferred applicant to whom you can make a prompt offer but don't make the mistake of turning down any other suitable person who could be kept in reserve. Your first choice may refuse your offer and you will need the second in line.

You've found the person you want – but recruiting hasn't finished!

This sounds like a contradiction but it all depends on what you mean by recruit. The effective leader will regard recruitment as completed when the new employee is not only physically present but integrated into the team and productive. This will not be the case on day one and further work is needed. A planned and monitored induction programme will do the trick and, if properly carried out, will also reduce the likelihood of the recruit resigning at an early stage. Studies have shown that a large proportion of resignations take place within the first six months of a job and they are often the result of inadequate induction.

■ *Induction*

The first few days in a new job can be a stressful time, especially for young people and most especially for those taking on their first job. The newcomer will want to do well and feel part of things but is faced with a strange environment which may seem unfriendly and even threatening. Your role as leader is to create a friendly and welcoming environment so that the initial enthusiasm of the recruit is encouraged and not eroded away.

The following steps should be taken:

1 Make sure that the receptionist is aware that the recruit is arriving and where he or she is to go.

If a recruit finds that no one seems to know who he or she is or what they are there for it is tantamount to saying, 'You are of no importance and we don't really care if you are here or not.' Motivation and commitment will be killed stone dead within minutes of the recruit stepping through the door.

2 See that arrangements are made to conduct the recruit to the appropriate place without delay. Being kept waiting is also demotivating.

3 Ensure that other members of the team are informed of the newcomer's arrival and are ready to give a warm welcome.

The team leader will ideally be the first person to meet and greet the recruit and express pleasure that he or she has started.

4 Provide a clean and tidy workplace with all the necessary tools, books, equipment or whatever in good condition. One company always gave the oldest typewriter to the newest typist or secretary thus ensuring that they were made to feel inferior right from the start!

5 Have someone ready to show the recruit round and to explain arrangements for meals, where the lavatories are, how to get a cup of coffee, how to requisition stationery and so on.

The same person could be appointed as a 'buddy' to help the newcomer with any difficulties over the first two or three weeks.

6 See that there is some work ready for the newcomer or, if necessary, a training plan ready to be put into action. If the recruit is left hanging about with little or nothing to do during the first day or two it will be demotivating and a waste of the salary you are paying. Get the newcomer active as soon as possible.

7 Check that the recruit was given all necessary information about working hours, pension scheme, holidays, sick pay and so on. All of this should have been explained before or at the time an offer was made but something may have been overlooked.

Much of this list will be dealt with during the first day but the process of induction should continue for some time.

■ *The next few days*

As the team leader, you should arrange to have a chat with the recruit after two or three days have elapsed and later at weekly intervals for, say, three weeks.

Those sessions can be used to:

- Confirm that the recruit has no problems, is happy and settling in
- Give the recruit an opportunity to make any points he or she wishes
- Further explain the job and how it fits in to the wider scheme
- Check that any training is achieving the right result and that the training programme is being adhered to
- Explain and discuss work standards and objectives and identify any additional knowledge that the recruit may need in order to work effectively.

All of this is important in terms of the recruit's contentment and in turn the recruit's contribution to the team. The process may have to go on for some time, possibly with a reduced frequency of discussions but until the recruit is no longer identifiable as a newcomer.

Use checklists

The conduct of the induction programme can be best controlled by using checklists and ticking off the completed items. This will help to ensure that nothing is overlooked in the hustle and bustle of daily activities. It is also a good tip to have a deputy ready to take over in the event that the normally responsible person is absent. Your checklist could look something like the one on the next page.

A copy of the checklist should be provided to all concerned, including the recruit. The recruit will then know what he or she will be involved in and will have another confirmation that 'somebody cares'. When the programme is completed and the employee is clearly an established member of the team then he or she will no longer be a recruit and the job of recruiting will be finished.

INDUCTION CHECKLIST – JOHN SMITH			
		Responsible	*Deputy*
Day 1	Reception informed	Jones	Green
	Buddy appointed	Jones	Green
	Workplace ready	Jones	Green
	Introductions	Jones	Green
	Initial explanation of work	Brown	Green
	Administration – Salaries/P45	Brown	Green
	– Safety rules		
	– Meals		
Day 2	On-job-training Part I	Brown	Green
	Visit to factory	Brown	Green
Day 3	On-job-training Part II	Brown	Green
	Review with team leader	Brown	Green

. . . and so on.

■ Summary of main points

1 Successful recruitment (finding someone who 'fits in' with the team as well as having the right skills) is another key part of effective leadership.

2 Someone's departure should not, automatically, be regarded as a case for recruitment. There may be an opportunity to reorganise work in some way which makes replacement unnecessary and improves the efficiency of the team.

3 If you must recruit start looking in-house. A promotion or transfer may offer advantages and be motivating. It can also be cheaper even if someone has to be recruited at a lower level to replace the promoted employee.

4 Before recruiting, work out a job description. This will be the foundation of any later advertising and leads to the preparation of a 'person profile' describing the type of person you will look for.

5 Beware of the traps such as demanding unnecessarily high qualifications or restricting the age range.

6 Fitting in is vitally important. It takes just one misfit to ruin a good team.

7 Carry out an analysis of the characteristics of your team to find out more objectively what sort of person will be compatible.

8 Use your team members to help you find the right person. They may know someone and are unlikely to recommend a misfit.

9 Part of the search for a recruit can be handled for you by an agency but watch the costs and check them out before signing a contract.

10 If you advertise think carefully about:

- The medium (will your ideal person see it?)
- The wording (it should be friendly and clear, limited to essential information, and describe the job properly)
- The rewards and conditions (don't be coy about salary levels)
- Making it easy for people to apply for the job you are offering. The method should be easy and the invitation friendly.

11 Sort out the applications methodically and *quickly*. Making people wait a long time for a reply can damage you and them and can create enemies you can do without.

12 Involve some (or maybe all) of your team in sorting out a shortlist for interview. The views of your team will help to ensure a fit and to avoid the effects of prejudice and stereotyping.

13 Think carefully and *prepare* for the interview. Have your questions worked out in advance and bone up on the applicant's details.

14 Arrange the time for the interview to suit the applicant. Make arrangements for the applicant to be properly received and treated with consideration and courtesy.

15 The team leader should conduct the interview but it will help if other team members are involved. Consider an informal 'interview' when the team and the applicant can meet on a social basis. This also helps to avoid the misfit problem.

16 Act fast after the interviews – don't keep the applicants waiting. Avoidable delay is not fair to the applicants and you may lose your preferred choice who could go elsewhere in the meantime.

17 The recruitment process has not ended when an offer has been made and accepted. A thoroughly planned induction programme must be carried out. This will motivate the newcomer and make him or her more productive more quickly.

8 What Now?

You have read in the previous chapters the fundamental requirements for effective leadership. You have, by doing so, started or continued a process of learning which should never come to an end. There may be areas of activity which you would like to explore further and to delve into in more detail. Much depends on your circumstances and the particular demands which your job makes on you.

This chapter gives you some ideas for continuing the learning process and provides sources of more information which you may feel you need. However, improving your effectiveness as a leader must always be founded on a particular form of practice.

■ **'Analysed practice'**

Practising leadership could be limited to just being a leader, trying to remember to motivate, set objectives and the like and leaving it at that, but you will achieve much more by adopting a disciplined and regular analysis of both successes and failures. How you do this is up to you but something along these lines will help:

1 Make some notes as you go through each month recording significant events on which your leadership skills had a bearing. The notes, which will be used to jog your memory later, need only be brief, for example:

- Quality meeting inconclusive, Smith and Jones at loggerheads

- OJT programme for George completed, results look good
- Delivery failure to ABC Ltd
- Brown left folder of urgent invoices unfinished, not noticed for three days
- Caught up on timetable to install new machinery.

Board-level or other more senior people might record something along these lines:

- Draft of report for shareholders two days late
- Budget analysis showed variances which should not have occurred
- New product launch on time and good response to press releases.

2 At month-end (or any other convenient but *regular* time) look at each note and analyse the causes.

For instance:

- Why was the quality meeting inconclusive?

    Poor chairmanship?

    No agenda?

    No clear purpose?

- Why were Smith and Jones at loggerheads?

    A communication failure?

    Conflicting objectives?

- Why was George's OJT programme so successful?

    Good planning?

    Implementation programme adhered to?

    George well motivated?

An honest answer to such questions can tell you why you went wrong and why you succeeded.

Actions (or inactions) which caused a problem can now be

consciously remedied and those which worked well for you can be repeated.

A disciplined approach such as this can have a marked effect on performance. Being human we will make mistakes but without some kind of formal analysis we will be likely not to think consciously about the reasons for them. The same applies to our successes, some of which we will take for granted.

▌ More to read

If you want to learn more about specific techniques some of these books may help you:

Goal Analysis by *Robert Mager* (Kogan Page)
deals with the problem of setting objectives and measuring the results when no clear (for example, mathematical) values can be applied. You may find some of Mager's examples and language need a little translation from the U.S. to the European but it is a useful read for all that.

The Best Person for the Job by *Malcolm Bird* (Piatkus Books)
gives more detail on recruitment, interviewing and other selection techniques. There is also a chapter on induction and another which deals with the problem of absenteeism.

Ideas for Enterprising Managers by *Matthew Archer* (Mercury)
provides a wide range of ideas for the leaders seeking to improve the effectiveness of their teams. How to give your operation a 'health check', how to get the structure right and how to solve complicated problems are among the subjects covered.

Better Communication Skills for Work by *Melanie Kelcher* (BBC Books)
provides a self-help course in improving your verbal and oral skills. This book, written by an author experienced in adult literacy training, is particularly suited to leaders who have had only a limited basic education and are now encountering problems as responsibility increases.

How to Make Your Training Pay by *Malcolm Bird* (Business Books) shows how training can be used to improve the team and how to go about it. How to link training and appraisal schemes, training and delegation, do-it-yourself training methods and how to check the results are all covered.

The Renewal Factor by *Robert H. Waterman Jr* (Bantam Press) is a readable commentary on the experiences of many leaders in a wide range of organisations. Waterman, co-author of the well-known book *In Search of Excellence,* talks about setting direction, the use of 'what-if' scenarios, identifying the really important issues, how to increase capabilities and much more of interest to leaders.

You may want to look at what more of the management gurus have to say, even if only for general interest. A good starting point is:

Guide to the Management Gurus by *Carol Kennedy* (Business Books)
This book summarises the views of thirty-three of the great theorists. This is a good book to dip into as a thought-provoker.

You may, having read this book, want to go to the sources and read something by one or other of the gurus included. There is one book which really should be on every leader's bookshelf.

The Human Organization by *Rensis Likert* (McGraw-Hill)
This book, in which Likert describes the characteristics of effective organisations and how successful leaders work, was published in 1967. It is still in print but rather expensive: a browse round the second-hand bookshops could be time well spent.

Another and much shorter book which gives us all something to think about is:

Leadership is not a Bowler Hat by *Peter J. Prior* (David and Charles)
should be read as a complement to the words of the gurus. This is out of print but worth searching for. Peter Prior wrote the book as a result of his chairmanship of Bulmers and it reflects the experiences of a hands-on leader. Prior led his company through a long period of growth and profit improvement so he is worth listening to.

Another book which complements the gurus is:

On Becoming a Leader by *Warren Bennis* (Business Books)
While Bennis is a guru himself he has based this book on
interviews with famous leaders and argues against the notion that
leaders are born.

The Iacocca Management Technique by *Maynard M. Gordon*
(Bantam Books)
is an interesting description of top-level leadership. Iacocca took
over Chairmanship of troubled Chrysler and the book describes
how he tackled this 'mission impossible'.

Styles of management such as the dynamic entrepreneur and the
finicky bureaucrat are examined in
Gods of Management by *Charles Handy* (Business Books)
This entertaining treatment is a warning to those leaders who
might be prone to going too far in adopting a particular style.

Something to look at

There are a number of companies offering training videos on
subjects ranging over just about every aspect of business. Some of
these videos are excellent as a source of good ideas while some
leave much to be desired.

The good videos illustrate the use of leadership skills in situations
which real people can relate to. Ideally the video will be based on
the sort of position that a leader can find himself or herself in and
show how to act to avoid problems, solve problems or make good
use of an opportunity.

A company which offers some really helpful and informative
videos on leadership is Longman Training (Longman House, Burnt
Mill, Harlow, Essex CM20 2JE).

Among the items in Longman's catalogue are:

- *The Successful Supervisor*
  This thirty-minute video tells the story of a badly led
  woman who is pitchforked into her first leadership
  position. She takes over a mess which includes a war
  going on between the people she is responsible for. She

makes a series of fundamental mistakes leading to a crisis situation.

With some help she adopts a different approach, makes use of communication and other techniques, and gets things right. The film ends with a somewhat Utopian state of affairs but this adds to the entertainment value of the video and reinforces the information given.

This video should be required viewing both for those being prepared for leadership and for existing leaders at all levels. Chairmen of great enterprises can also learn from this video and the word 'supervisor' in the title should not put them off.

Ideally, *The Successful Supervisor* should be seen two or three times and discussed in order to get the most out of it. There are so many lessons to be learned that they may not all sink in with one viewing. The same applies to:

- *Time to Think*, which is often considered to be a classic.

This video was designed to illustrate the best practices of good time-management but it also illustrates very well some bad and good leadership techniques. Among other things, the video demonstrates the need for delegation (and how to go about it); the importance of organising work and the team; and the impact that the leader can have on team morale.

The film shows clearly the adverse effect of a workaholic leader on his team and how his involvement in detail and lack of clear objectives reduce his effectiveness and damage his reputation. Although the leader and the team are entirely fictional the comments and reactions of the various characters could well be taken from real life. Viewers will recognise the situations illustrated and the solutions to the problems are well presented and of practical value.

There are other videos in the Longman range which will help leaders wanting to improve their performances. They include:

- *The Art of Team Building*, which illustrates how to weld the people into a team, the leader's role as part of the team and in setting objectives.

- *The Pursuit of Efficiency*, starring Penelope Keith, uses real-life cases to show how to reduce waste of resources and time and how to get things done more efficiently.

- *Meeting the Meeting Challenge* tackles the problems of handling conflict and reluctance to participate at meetings. This video also deals with the important matter of obtaining everyone's commitment in a group discussion.

- *The Art of Interviewing* covers all the recruitment essentials for making a reliable assessment of a job applicant.

Some or perhaps all of these videos may help you to plug any gaps in your range of leadership skills or to act as a 'refresher' to get you back to thinking about the basics and how you measure up.

Courses – formal and less formal

In addition to the do-it-yourself approach using books and videos, leadership training is available through a number of training courses. These break down into two broad categories: public courses and in-house private courses.

■ Public courses

These are offered by many organisations whose advertisements can be found in the business press. Some offer their services via mail shots to former and prospective clients.

The quality of such offerings is variable and needs careful checking-out before parting with your hard-earned cash. Advice may be available from your trade association or from reputable organisations such as the Institute of Personnel Management or the British Institute of Management.

One dependable source of training is the Industrial Society (Peter Runge House, 3 Carlton House Terrace, London SW1Y 3DG), which offers courses on 'Action Centred Leadership'. This approaches leadership from the viewpoint that the effective leader will need to balance the needs of:

- The team
- The individuals

and • Achieving the task.

A telephone call to the Industrial Society (071–839 4300) could put you on the right track.

One advantage of an external course is the chance for you to meet leaders from other companies and industries. The sharing of experiences and ideas can be valuable – as is the discovery that other people have the same problems and worries as you do.

The disadvantage is that the course may not suit your particular needs: perhaps only parts of it are relevant to you. Make careful enquiries into the course objectives and content as well as the quality.

Be wary of organisations offering extravagant claims. No one can turn you into a brilliant leader in six hours. Such claims are often made for courses which owe more to show business than serious attention to workplace problems. You will learn nothing from strobe lights, music and a man in a pink suit trying to imitate Billy Graham.

■ Private courses

Training can be provided in-house by training consultants who will tailor courses to suit your particular needs. If you have a number of people requiring leadership training this can be a cost-effective method. There will be no time lost on travelling or hotel expenses to contend with as long as you can provide a suitable room on your own premises. A good trainer will check what you need before you start and structure the training to give you a value for money deal.

Such training can be obtained from management consultants, often linked to some form of management consultancy project. There are a number of well-known big names in the training business but you may prefer a smaller supplier.

Smaller organisations are often easier to work with, have lower overheads and more readily develop a personal relationship with you and your people.

A small supplier you might contact is Development Partnerships (tel: 0488-648278) which, in addition to conference-room-type training, also offers outdoor training.

A breath of fresh air
Becoming an effective leader is as much concerned with learning about yourself as about how to relate to your team. Both can be learned outside the office or factory.

Development Partnerships can provide you and your colleagues with an outdoor course using exercises lasting from about forty minutes to a number of hours. They are designed to reflect the variety of situations faced at work but, by stripping away the workplace environment with its politics and culture, the course enable trainees to get to the guts of leadership and team work.

A typical programme would be designed to give participants opportunities:

1 To receive feedback on their behaviour when leading and being a member of a small group.

2 To observe and to give feedback to a small group.

3 To identify new skills, and to develop and practise them within a supportive and encouraging environment.

4 To practise the essential skills necessary to lead a small group successfully.

5 To develop their skills in being successful group members.

6 To practise skills relevant to their own development.

Achieving these objectives does not involve testing your physical strength or endurance so don't feel that you need to be an Olympic athlete to take part. The exercises are designed to be serious but fun – with a lot learned at the end of it all.

Another provider of leadership training in the great outdoors is the Outward Bound Trust (Chestnut Field, Regent Place, Rugby CV21 2PJ, Tel: 0788 560423).

The trust offers a five-day Effective Teamwork course at centres at Loch Eil, Eskdale and Ullswater. The aims of these courses are:

- To help the individual identify and develop teamwork skills.

- To examine how a team can achieve results by harnessing the knowledge, skills and resources at its disposal.

- To allow team members to experience a number of roles, in particular those of leader/doer/influencer/supporter.

This course is not just a matter of rushing around the countryside doing energetic things. Participants will finish the course by completing their own action plan and agreeing guidelines for their continuing development with Outward Bound tutors. The course includes workshop sessions, reviews and feedback. Their 'How effective have we been?' approach provides the opportunity to draw practical conclusions from the practical work.

The Trust also offers tailor-made courses for groups of eight to twelve people at five residential centres. In partnership with you the Trust will develop a training package which can include pre- and post-course elements. Examples of such programmes carried out for UK companies include:

- Teambuilding – understanding the dynamics of risk taking in a team context

- Development of managerial skills through team activities

- Refinement of teamwork and leadership skills

- Leadership development

- Team development – breaking down communication barriers

- Preparation for becoming first-level managers; personal effectiveness within a group.

Full details of courses available can be obtained by contacting the Trust's Marketing Manager.

Meanwhile, back in the classroom . . .

Indoor and in-house courses are available from a wide range of suppliers. Such 'classroom' work is not, of course, an alternative to outdoor leadership training. The two are complementary.

MaST Organisation Ltd (Hermitage House, Bath Road, Taplow, Maidenhead, Berkshire SL6 0AR, Tel. 0628 784062) will review your training needs and provide courses to meet them.

The Industrial Society (Peter Runge House, 3 Carlton House Terrace, London SW1 3DG, Tel. 071 839 4300) also provides leadership training. Their course in Action Centred Leadership may be particularly useful to you. This courses addresses the leader's responsibilities in respect to the task to be achieved, the team and the individual.

What's in It for You?

Maslow talked about our need for self-fulfilment – and nothing equals the pleasure of finding it.

Success as a leader is self-evident in a happy, co-operative and relaxed team which achieves its objectives. This success creates a whopping sense of self-fulfilment and this is worth working for.

Neither you nor any of your friends and colleagues will have been born as a leader and you will need to learn and practise the necessary skills. Don't despair if you make the odd mistake (we all do). All the ideas in this book are based on real-life observation and experience. Choose the ones which suit you and your circumstances best and put them to use.

Above all consult your team. Be guided by them – and enjoy the self-fulfilment which inevitably follows. Good luck and good leading!